CAMBRIDGE AND STOURBRIDGE FAIR

Honor Ridout

Blue Ocean Publishing

Cambridge and Stourbridge Fair

Published by Blue Ocean Publishing

St John's Innovation Centre

Cambridge CB4 0WS

United Kingdom

www.blueoceanpublishing.biz

Typesetting by Spitfire Design, Upminster

Printed by CLE Print Ltd, St Ives.

A catalogue record for this book is available from the British Library. ISBN 978-1-907527-01-2

First published in the United Kingdom in 2011 by Blue Ocean Publishing.

Contents

1	The Beginnings	1
2	Townsmen and Scholars	7
3	Setting up the Fair	15
4	Life at the Fair	21
5	*Come buy!*	31
6	Food at the Fair	53
7	Entertainment	57
8	Trials and Tribulations	70
9	Owning Booths	76
10	The Decline of the Fair	83

Appendix: Visiting Traders at Stourbridge Fair 1745–1802   92

Sources and select bibliography   95

Index   97

Money Conversion: what the pounds, shillings and
pence were worth   99

Thanks and Acknowledgements   100

Maps:

Location of the Fair   iv

Centre of Cambridge in 1798   9

Map of the Fair 1725   17

Plan of the Fair: remembered c.1820   81

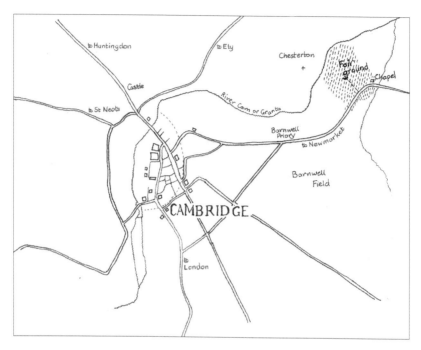

Location of the Fair

Leper Chapel, 1818

1 The Beginnings

September was the best month in Cambridge because it was Fair month. For centuries, Cambridge people relished this occasion to make money, to meet old friends, to enjoy special dinners and first class entertainments. The general buzz and excitement enlivened everyone, rich and poor.

The beginnings of Cambridge's once-famous Fair are lost about 800 years ago. They may go back further. The first record is one bald statement: in 1211 the right to run a fair each 14th September was granted by royal charter to the Leper Hospital of Cambridge. Was that the beginning, or simply a legal recognition of an established event? We'll probably never know. At any rate, the charter ensured that the religious men who looked after the little hospital could collect all the rents and tolls from the traders, to apply to the welfare of their patients.

Trade was the essential purpose of the Fair and remained so for its active life. The location was superb. The Hospital (of which we know almost nothing) had been set up beside the main east-bound road, on the furthest boundary of the Cambridge fields. The lepers were not to live close to any other residents, but they, or their carers, could beg for alms from travellers passing by. Their eastern boundary, and that of the Cambridge fields, was a small stream, crossed by a bridge over which cattle could safely pass. Hence it was called Steers Bridge. Northwards across the common pastures was the river, a vital channel for the trade that had created Cambridge itself. From the Hospital could be seen the boats, laden with grain, wool, timber and other essential commodities. There was little difficulty in getting produce offloaded near the Hospital and dragged up to the precincts. So both road and river served the Fair with goods and customers.

Annual fairs were a growing trend around 1200. Although most people could provide for their basic needs from their own produce, landowners often had a surplus to dispose of, and a hankering for finer things produced in other parts or even abroad. A town like Cambridge, growing as a market centre to redistribute goods in its own area, had a very mixed economy. The large fields, one either side of the town, provided barley, wheat, rye, peas and beans that were the staple of life, and plenty of grazing for cattle, sheep and pigs. Even the town's craftsmen might also keep animals in barns behind their houses, and own a few strips of land in the fields. It was commonplace then, and for centuries to come, to meet animals being driven through the streets. On the other hand, a wide range of crafts were practised, from the humdrum shoemaking, baking and blacksmithing to the luxury goldsmith's work. Cambridge was a growing centre, and the benefits of trade meant that the richest men could afford luxuries both local and imported.

At about the same time that the lepers' fair was chartered, the leading residents were negotiating with the King or his officers to achieve a form of self-government. They wanted, and got, the right to choose their own mayor and council, and to have power over the market. It's rather odd that they didn't establish their own official fair in Cambridge at the same time. It was a valuable asset, one every town at that time sought to establish, as a means to greater wealth and prestige. Three annual fairs were confirmed and chartered in Cambridge: the Midsummer Fair belonged to the Priory at Barnwell, the August Garlic Fair to the nuns of St Radegund, and the Steresbridge Fair to the Leper Hospital. The Corporation got the rights to Reach Fair, held in May at the little hamlet on the edge of the Fens. (Today only two fairs survive: Midsummer Fair as a large funfair, and Reach Fair revived from near extinction since the May Day Bank Holiday was created in 1978.)

It's not clear why Steresbridge (only much later called Stourbridge) outstripped the other fairs. They all shared the geographical benefits of the river trade and the main roads that brought the Midlands–East Anglia and North–London traffic close to or through Cambridge. Cambridgeshire was a convenient two-day ride for smart London merchants seeking to expand their trade. We know nothing of Stourbridge's early years. Was there an entrepreneurial individual behind it – one man who fixed the charter, first raising the necessary gold to pay the King (and his officials) for the privilege? Perhaps the right words in the right ears were needed to get key merchants to come to Steresbridge rather than to any other fair in the area. (The growth of Stourbridge corresponded with the decline of the great Easter Fair at St Ives, which had attracted foreign merchants and provided quantities of luxury fabric for the royal wardrobe.)

Somehow, Stourbridge became the place to go. Royal records show that around 1250, King Henry III had his officers buy cloth at the Fair. Later, in the 1280s, his son Edward I was rebuilding Cambridge castle, and iron hinges and window bars, fetters and chains were bought at Stourbridge.

By 1279, the Leper Hospital had ceased to function. The Warden was accused that 'he did not maintain any lepers in that hospital as he ought of right to do'. The Fair, on the other hand, was so successful that the Cambridge Corporation stepped in to run it. Sadly for historians, the Corporation records for this period were not as well kept as the royal ones. There's nothing to tell us how the Fair was run then: the pitches allocated, the dues collected, law and order maintained. For that information we have to wait.

Cambridge's river trade passing Chesterton church

It's not too surprising that little information remains about the Fair from this period, when few people could write. What survive are documents dealing with money or with law, and from both there are snippets about Stourbridge. The household accounts of Dame Alice de Bryene from Acton in Suffolk (40 miles from Cambridge) reveal that she or her steward came to buy fish, (dried, salted and fresh,) spices, currants and raisins and equipment for her kitchen. King's Hall in Cambridge (a forerunner of Trinity College) bought similar provisions, including saffron, almonds and mustard-seed. Religious houses (good record keepers) from Thetford to Bursted, Oxfordshire, used the Fair. Cloth, timber and iron sales continued to flourish and new commodities arrived when they became fashionable. As part of the ordering of the Fair, the different commodities were sold in their own areas or rows.

By the late 1300s, the plots along the main paths in the Fair had become defined and 'owned' for the duration of the Fair. You had to be a freeman of the Borough to own a plot. By 1405, it was laid down that a freeman could have one booth free of any dues to the Corporation. If he owned any more, he had to pay the fees. He could hand on his booth or booths to another freeman by gift or sale. If he did that, the change of ownership had to be registered through the Corporation. These ownerships were respected through to the final decline of the Fair.

While the Corporation was dealing with all these matters, a devastating change had come about in its powers within the Borough. In 1209, some scholars arrived from Oxford and never quite returned there. Within a few years, they were recognised as a new university. Relations with Cambridge town soon became uneasy over the prices charged for lodgings, food and fuel. Despite the attempts of the King to keep the peace by instituting joint committees of University and Corporation to deal with the problems, there were sporadic outbreaks of violence. These culminated in 1381 in Cambridge's own version of the Peasants' Revolt. Not all who revolted were peasants, and there was strong anti-University feeling that was expressed in the seizing and burning of University documents. Punishment was swift and uncompromising. The University was confirmed in important privileges over the townsmen: rights in the market to inspect the quality and price of goods and to check the weights and measures used. Public entertainments were subject to the Chancellor's approval, to prevent the students being distracted from their studies. These rights extended to Stourbridge Fair, so both town and University authorities were involved in the jurisdiction.

A major event in the Fair's history occurred in 1538 when the King's Attorney General challenged the Corporation to prove its right to run the Fair (and to collect the considerable sums of money it brought in). The town had no such proof, and was faced with a swingeing fine of 1000 marks (£666 6s 8d) (six shillings and eightpence) which would pay for the rights. The horrified Corporation took steps to get the money raised, but it took a long time. It seems the Fair went on running as before. It was far too valuable to national commerce to close down, or to risk transferring the operation to less experienced hands.

A few years later, under national legislation which abolished small chapels, the Leper Chapel became the property of the Crown, and the chaplain was pensioned off. To the Corporation's further annoyance, the University also decided to put in a claim to run the Fair. The matter remained unsettled for 40 years. Finally, Queen Elizabeth decided in the Corporation's favour, and awarded a Charter in 1589. Nevertheless, the University kept the rights established in 1381, and both town and University had to proclaim their separate regulations at the opening of the Fair. The Charter stated that Stourbridge 'far surpassed the greatest and most celebrated fairs of all England, whence great benefit had resulted to the merchants of the whole kingdom'. It added that Cambridge had been able to pay the greater part of its taxes through the revenues and 'maintained the town in its ways, streets, ditches and other burthens'. The goods traded included 'salt-fish, butter, cheese, honey, flax, hemp, pitch, tar and all other wares and merchandises'. The goods did change over time, but the Fair was secure.

These early records have no need to describe the physical appearance of the Fair, so they don't. Fortunately, in the late 1600s, the national expansion of trade seized the public imagination. An interest in things mercantile began to be a fashion and, for the first time, people published descriptions of Stourbridge Fair. One of the first, a descriptive poem by Thomas Hill, was written solely for gentlemen and scholars, as it was in Latin, and included all sorts of allusions to Classical literature. By contrast, *A Step to Stir-Bitch-Fair*, by Ned Ward, was humorous, and made great fun of the less respectable aspects of fair-going. An anonymous poem, *The Refusal of the Hand* (alluding to Pope's *Rape of the Lock*), again told a light-hearted tale of a young girl returning to Cambridge for the Fair. Then, in 1724, Daniel Defoe published his *Tour through the Whole Island of Great Britain* which included (at last!) a substantial description of the Fair, its layout, the goods sold and the entertainments enjoyed. (A mere half page dealt with the town and the University.) The description was so useful it was freely borrowed by other writers for the next 50 years. A few years after Defoe, local newspapers were set up, and the *Cambridge Journal and*

Weekly Flying Press, the *Cambridge Chronicle* and the *Cambridge Intelligencer* provided news, editorial comment and advertisements for businesses and shows at the Fair.

Over these centuries, a stream of casual references in plays, verse, letters and accounts witnesses the importance of Stourbridge Fair in the national economy and consciousness. It was a marker in space and time until, at last, greater movements in the national economy moved business to other places.

Steresbregge. The earliest name referred to the cattle or steers driven across the bridge. (No name for the stream itself is mentioned, though it's later Coldham's Brook.) All spelling is phonetic, so there are variants: Sterisbrig, Sturesbrig, etc.

Stirbrigge.

By the sixteenth century, the middle s is usually left out. The bridge becomes irrelevant, and local speech goes on to omit the letter r. By the eighteenth century it's down to

Stirbitch.

Tales arise to account for the Fair being named after an instruction to a dog. But even the *Cambridge Chronicle* uses this spelling until the 12th September 1778. In the next edition, the 19th September, every reference to the Fair has been reset as

Stourbridge.

In 1779, the editor reverts to Stirbitch. By 1781, there's a compromise: Sturbidge. In the end, local historians decree that the original name must have been Stourbridge, as the stream was probably the Stour: reasonable, but wrong.

The local pronunciation is **Sturbridge.**

---

2 Townsmen and Scholars

Despite their many recorded quarrels, most of the time the town and the University worked together – because they had to. The scholars depended on the town for food and personal services. Their cooks, porters, tailors, barbers and washerwomen were all townsfolk. The townsfolk made money out of the students, some of whom (though not all) came from wealthy families and had plenty to spend. Townsmen and gownsmen lived cheek by jowl in the compact town hemmed in by its great fields. As the number of scholars increased over the centuries, the custom they provided became a more and more significant part of the tradesmen's business. When the students went home in the summer, it was noted the townsmen had clean hands and clean aprons, and little to do until the Fair in September and the new University term. The exception might be provided by a new college wing or even a new court, which kept the carpenters, bricklayers, stonemasons, plumbers and glaziers busy for months.

Cambridge remained a compact place until about 1800. The river, in several channels, formed the western and northern boundaries, with an outlying spur of settlement flowing up and down Castle Street. Around the east and south of the town was the King's Ditch, probably dating from Saxon times. It served to regulate the entry of loaded vehicles rather than to keep out armies. Some houses straggled along the roads in and out: Wall's Lane (modern King Street), Preachers' Street (St Andrew's) and Trumpington Road. In the Middle Ages, with the population well under 5,000, the town was reasonably spacious. There were some comfortably-off residents, owning properties in and outside the town, with business interests in local commodities or imports. There were craftsmen and tradesmen in all the various foodstuffs, clothing trades, metal and building works. Some of them would have lived in smart houses, like the medieval frontages we still have in Bridge Street. By 1500, that would have been replicated along the main streets throughout town. Behind lay yards with stores, cattlesheds and haylofts, and gardens with vegetables and fruit trees. Taller buildings in timber with overhanging jetties, went up in the sixteenth century. Most of the streets were very narrow, which made driving wagons through the town and in and out of the yards a very skilful business. The satirical Ned Ward suggested that even two wheelbarrows passing each other could cause a traffic jam.

Besides its 15 churches, the medieval town contained four friaries, a priory, a convent and several smaller religious houses. These communities were also a prominent part of the daily scene, until closed down. The nuns of St Radegund, always a small number, had virtually disappeared when they were closed in 1496, but the most stunning event was the closure of the friaries and the priory in 1539. The King removed the valuable property, and the sites became quarries (with and without permission) until most were acquired for colleges.

The gradual increase in the number of students provided work for more folk in town, and this increase peaked in the 1620s. Thereafter, there was a slow overall decline in student numbers, until the nineteenth century. However, the general trade of the area helped support the town, although Cambridge was never wealthy enough to put up the fine public buildings and walks that other towns achieved in the eighteenth century. In 1734, the young Thomas Gray described the town in a letter to a friend as 'like a spider, with a nasty lump in the middle and half a dozen scambling long legs'. He was aiming to amuse, but he wasn't the only person with that view. The half-timbered medieval houses that were state of the art in 1500 were not so pretty by 1700, and few people had caught up with the new fashion for brick with sash windows. By then, the medieval population had perhaps doubled and, with the expansion of the colleges, was a snug fit between the river and the ditch. Gardens were fewer and small houses

---

Centre of Cambridge in 1798, mapped by William Custance

Cambridge at the moment before its expansion beyond its medieval bounds. The market is confined to an L-shape radiating from Hobson's Conduit (B). The Shire Hall built in 1749 on the place of the medieval Shambles (q) obscures the Guildhall immediately to the south(r). (The houses between the Corn Market and Great St Mary's church were partly burnt down and the rest demolished in 1849.) Houses line the road in front of King's College, with the Provost's Lodge and the Choir School, and the Senate House (S) is here only 70 years old.

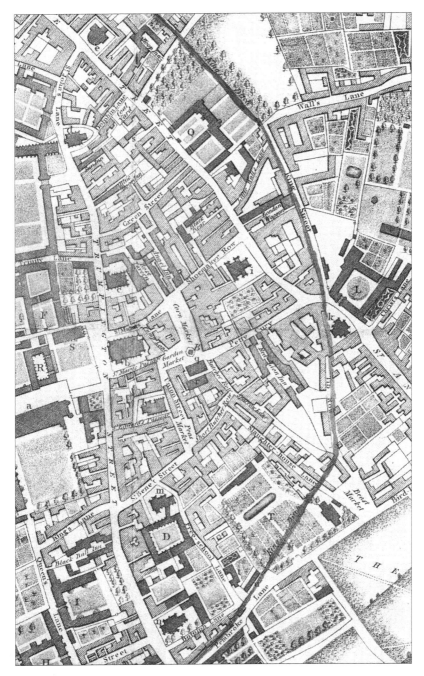

were crammed into the back yards. By the end of the eighteenth century, the population was around 9,000 and in need of more space.

Local organisation changed very little over these centuries. People were often identified by the parish in which they lived, for the church was not only where they met their neighbours every Sunday for religious observance. From Tudor times onwards, it was the focus of social organisation. The better-off parishioners took turns in filling the roles of churchwarden, overseer of the poor, and constable, which meant collecting rates from fellow parishioners to support the church and its property, to support the poorest in the community and to maintain very basic elements of law and order. If you were poor and desperate, you went to one of these men in your parish to beg a few pence for coals or new clothes or medicines.

The ordering of the Borough as a whole was in the hands, officially, of the mayor, bailiffs and burgesses. The burgesses did not include all the inhabitants, but only the freemen, of whom there were about 200 – a small proportion of the population. To become a freeman, it was necessary to be the eldest son of a freeman, or his apprentice, or to get the Corporation to admit you for a fee. In return for this status, you had the right to vote for the town's MPs, the right to fill any of a number of official posts (unpopular – many new freemen paid again to be excused this privilege) and the right to be chosen one of the 24 common councilmen, and thence perhaps an alderman or even mayor. The mayor was obliged on election to kneel to the University authorities and to swear to uphold the University's privileges, which made embarrassingly public the true hierarchy in the town.

The other posts included the very important bailiffs, one for each ward of the town: Bridge, High, Market and Preachers (Preachers' Street, now St Andrew's Street). The bailiffs were responsible for collecting tolls and dues for the Corporation, particularly at the fairs. There are no recorded accounts of this money. Most of the income seems to have gone to pay the town's taxes to the King, with the residue (after their own expenses) spent providing official dinners, notably at the proclamations of the fairs and at Michaelmas, when the new mayor took office each year.

Three Crowns, Silver Street: typical of the prestige houses from about 1600 that survived into the nineteenth or even twentieth centuries
From Redfarn's Old Cambridge

Until the reform of corporations by Act of Parliament in the 1830s, town councils had few legal duties and could decide for themselves how much they contributed to the welfare of the townspeople. Householders were expected to keep the street clean in front of their own house, and to dispose of their own rubbish and to light the roadway outside when necessary. The Cambridge Corporation stepped in only when absolutely necessary. It paid a scavenger to clean up after the market, occasionally organised repaving of the most central streets and ordered other people to do their public duty of clearing up after themselves. The mayor and one or two aldermen were also Justices of the Peace, and held courts to deal with minor law-breaking.

The Corporation was still concerned with the market and the fairs, despite the University having the whip hand in regulating weights, measures and quality. The townspeople took any chance they could see to involve themselves where their interests were at stake. It was standard practice, backed by various laws, to limit market trading to set hours (marked by ringing a bell) and to the designated market area. Trading outside was condemned because it generally involved middle-men trying to buy up a commodity to force up the price (engrossing or forestalling), or to resell in the same market at a higher price (regrating). Ideally, the foodstuffs in the market were sold directly by the producer to the consumer, and the Corporation and the University wanted to keep it that way.

To manage the Fair, the Corporation found it convenient to hand over to a sub-committee called the Regulators, to act in matters of forfeited booths, placing of wares and general order. Six or eight, half aldermen, half common councilmen, were chosen on 16th August each year. To help them, they had the Redcoats (so called – presumably these were the harnessmen in their official coats) to round up malefactors and troublemakers, and the Lord Taps. This individual went about the Fair to check the quality of the beer (though how this fitted with the University's responsibilities for quality control isn't clear). To identify him, his official coat was hung about with taps or spigots, such as would be used in beer barrels.

While the Corporation was choosing and briefing the officers who were to run the Fair, the University similarly was deciding on its inspection team. The academics could not be expected to have any expertise in commodity quality, so they were paired with appropriate tradesmen from the town. The proctors, responsible for University discipline, were in command. They had the aid of the taxors, to deal with weights and measures violations, and some 'honest men' to help with the mundane jobs.

The proctors and taxors held their courts for the duration of the Fair, if necessary. The University's own scales and standard measures had to be taken along, and every year they brought out the battered volume in which the Fair courts' judgements were recorded. A new heading was written in large letters: **Nundinae Sturbrigiensis**. Below was a list of the commodities to be checked (also usually written in Latin – the University found it hard to work in English), with the names of the two inspectors against each. After that, the records were written as they happened, at the Fair, and the quality of the writing deteriorated sharply. But now everyone was ready for the first process – setting up the Fair.

The Nuttings, the Fair and the Map

1683   Walter Howland owns booths in Sturbridge Fair (in the right of his wife Elizabeth née Nutting), but chooses to live at his home, in Streatham in Surrey. He regularly pays Cambridge Corporation £6 fine to live away 3 years and keep his booths.

1692   Walter Howland dies. His widow, Elizabeth, keeps the booths, and goes on living in Streatham.

1711   Elizabeth Howland dies, and bequeaths her booths to her nephew, Howland Nutting, innkeeper of the Black Bear (in modern Market Passage) in Cambridge. Nutting pays £10 to be admitted as a freeman in order to possess the booths. He is concerned about the extent and boundaries of the booths, so has a surveyor measure all the booths at the Fair when it is set up in September. The results are neatly written down in a notebook. (Now in the Bowtell Collection, Downing College.)

1720   His son, Thomas, claims the freedom (as eldest son of a freeman). He is in business as a coal and corn merchant. The same year, he is chosen a common councilman and, in 1721, alderman. In August 1723, he is elected mayor for the next year. *[Fast-tracking, we might say!]*

1724   In May, Howland Nutting dies, bequeathing his booths to son, Thomas (though he requires Thomas to pay shares of the profits to his mother and his brothers).

         August: the Corporation registers concern about Fair holdings, and resolves to have an alphabetical register made of all the ownerships, and how held. Mayor Nutting is to find a surveyor to make the list and to pay him.

1725   Nutting is authorised to pay 'the Gent. that surveyed Stirbridge Fair' and made the plan thereof, six guineas. A copy of the map is placed on the wall in the mayor's booth. It survives until 1796 when workmen damage it during renovations. Fortunately, copies have already been made, and survive to the present day. These are the only precise maps of Sturbridge Fair we have.

The Proclamation of Sturbridge Fair

On St Bartholomew's Day, at the setting up of the Fair

1st   The King... by Mr Mayor .. doth straitly charge all coming to the Fair beginning on the Feast Day of St Bartholomew and continuing to the Feast Day of St Michael Archangel, to keep His Majesty's Peace

2nd   [Merchandise to be put to sale as and when appointed]

3rd   And that no Free Burgess or any other person having any right or authority to Build or Erect any Booth or Standings in the Fair Do let the same to any person or persons that shall sell therein any wares or Merchandises contrary to the Charters Customs and Ordinances on that Behalf made and Provided But that they observe and keep both in Building and letting of any of their Booths or Standings All and every the said Charters Customs and Ordinances Upon the several pains and Forfeitures in the Same Contained

And that no man Build any Booths or Cabbins upon the Causey or other Waste Ground in this Fair or make or set up any forehouses in any place within the said Fair which shall be Trenched in or stand further out than the Tilt of their Booths will stretch upon Pain of Imprisonment

And further that Free Burgesses here assembled do ride homewards in a Decent Manner not above two in a Rank upon Pain that everyone offending herein shall Forfeit three Shillings and Four Pence

And likewise give their attendance upon Mr Mayor in the Guildhall of this Town of Cambridge At the common Day there holden at two of the Clock this afternoon upon Pain of their Oaths

God Save the King

3 Setting up the Fair

On 24th August – St Bartholomew's Day – the Borough officers gathered together at the house of the mayor. They formed a long but neat procession, and took the road out to Barnwell and the Fair site. Tagging along came the carpenters and labourers with their tools, and wagonloads of timber and horse-hair cloths. Leaving the narrow town streets for the open fields, and the gentle rise from Butts Green, there was a little thrill of anticipation. At Barnwell, they passed the Abbey farmhouse, with perhaps a nod to the owner. He had to give up part of his fields for the Fair. Past the little cluster of houses and pubs, the procession rode into open country again. At the Coldhams Lane turn, they could see the Fairground ahead.

By the year 1700, a short row of small houses, timber with tiled roofs, stood on the left-handside of the road. They were Fair booths, at this point full of timber stored for the constructing of other booths. Their use as residences was strictly forbidden. Beyond, on both sides of the road, the crops had been harvested, and all that was left was stubble and stalks. Away to the left could be glimpsed the two-storey Mayor's House , and near the bottom of Garlic Row, Mr Alpha's house. On the right-handside, likewise, were two brick houses, one facing Garlic Row, the other further off. At Garlic Row, the procession halted and, having gathered in good order, all attended while the Proclamation was read. It established that the ground now belonged to the Fair, and that layout and construction could commence.

Once the procession had re-formed to return to town, the carpenters and their workmen could begin. The bailiffs had ultimate responsibility for the ground that was not to be built on, so presumably they lingered to see that the terms of the Proclamation were observed. The top of Garlic Row was identified by two boundary or dole stones, 24 ½ feet apart. The lower end, by the Common, also had a dole stone. Measurements could be taken from the various brick houses, from the gate onto the Common and, of course, from the Chapel. The position of each road and passage could be pegged out, and the precise position of every booth plotted.

For many of the workmen, the job was routine: they did it every year, unvaryingly. The main streets of the Fair were lined by owned plots, and the owners were responsible for getting their booths built. Some were lucky enough to get their timber stored on site, in one of the brick houses, or in the old Chapel. Some had to have it carted from town. Every carpenter in Cambridge was needed and they worked flat out, ignoring any other jobs that might be in hand. (A note one year from a Master of Jesus College lamented that alterations could not be done in college, for all the carpenters were at Stourbridge: 'It is their harvest,' he admitted.)

The booths on the principal streets were sturdy constructions of split deal boards, with pitched roofs covered in horse-hair cloth to keep out rain. The main part of each booth formed the shop, and was fitted with a counter and shelves. The overall booth sizes varied, from the tiny cheese booths, about six feet square, to the larger Garlic Row booths, which might be 14 feet deep by 24 feet long. On the front of each booth, an awning projected some six to ten feet, to protect the passing customer. On the back was constructed a bedroom, so that the booth-keeper and/or his servant could sleep on site.

One set of payments, from late in the Fair's history, details the labour involved in booth construction. A young heiress, Miss Tryce Mary Parratt, owned three booths on the west side of Garlic Row. Her agent submitted annual accounts (1764–1771) for the building of her booths. The construction was carried out by Thomas Smith, carpenter and auctioneer, and each year there were also bills for additional timber and for nails (supplied by the well-known ironfounders Finch). More hair-cloth for the roof was often needed, and fresh gravel was laid on the road before the booths. Six shillings was charged for wine for the three tenants and a modest 1s for ale for the workmen.

Besides the main streets, there were open areas of the Fair in which space was allocated by the bailiffs. These were for the bulky wholesale products that could be sold straight from the wagon or cart that brought them, or perhaps could be laid out on the ground. There were all manner of other stalls and tents, and pitches for pedlars, but no one troubled to describe them.

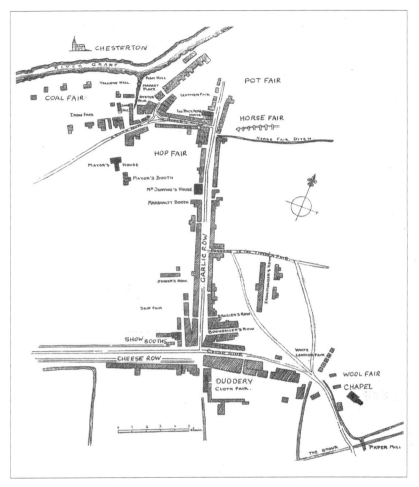

Map of Stourbridge Fair, based on the map and survey of 1725

The bailiffs had to be ever vigilant: there were always booth owners who wanted to spread themselves a little further, build their booths a little bigger and encroach on the bailiffs' 'waste' ground. It was a habit that sparked bitter resentment in the less enterprising merchants, and the Corporation had to deal with it: 'Whereas great complaint hath been made of the great disorder in Sturbridge faier ...' began the report, going on to describe how 'foreshows' and 'back grounds' had been established in front

17

of and behind booths where 'there hath never been any'. The bailiffs didn't know what to do about them, or how to charge them, so a sub-committee had to be set up to discuss the problem. Another ruse to gain more space, tried in 1630, was to build booths gable-end to the road. It was the way many houses in town were built and it meant the frontage stayed within the prescribed limits, while the booth could be extended at the back of the plot. The Corporation took a fierce line and required 'all booths in Garlick row and chepe side (except in the nether end of chepeside where the lynnen drapers stand) shall be built longwayes as they open in the fair and not with gable ends. If any shall hereafter build contrary to this order every such booth to be pulled down'. A firm response, though it doesn't explain why the linen drapers were excused!

The bailiffs were presumably responsible for other modifications to the site; rails or posts for the horse fair on the Common, were one simple requirement. A maypole was put up, a focal point for casual musicians and dancing, and a pulpit was erected in the Duddery for Sunday sermons. Although the sixteenth century Corporation approved repairs to a 'siegehouse' (siege = seat or throne) behind the Chapel, little or nothing more was recorded about meeting basic needs until one last tiny sketch of the Fair showed 'little edifices of general convenience'. Presumably the bailiffs put these up, with the necessary pits, seats, buckets or whatever. Commentators were far too coy to discuss these matters, so we don't know.

The bailiffs, carpenters and labourers had no time to dawdle over their work. Booths were fitted, their colourful signs hung up, and flags waved. As the wagon and cart-loads of goods entered the Fair grounds, they were charged a toll according to their kind by the bailiffs and their officers. Those not destined for the built booths were allocated their space, and put up their makeshift tents and shelters. Even the pedlars with backpacks or horsepacks had their space. All had to be ready for the official opening of the Fair on the 7th September.

Give us back our 11 days!

The dates of Sturbridge Fair are often confused because they changed in 1752. The British calendar was by that date 11 days adrift from the sun. To correct this (so that June 21st would once more be the longest day of the year and December 21st the shortest), 3rd – 13th were excised from September in 1752. It wouldn't do to shorten the periods within which financial debts had to be paid, so the financial year was shifted on 11 days on the calendar. That financial year, therefore, ran from Lady Day, 25th March, 1752 to April 6th 1753.

Similarly, from 1752 Sturbridge Fair was proclaimed on the 18th September and ended in October. 'Horse Fair Day', traditionally the original Fair day of the 14th September, became the 25th September.

The PROCESSION to the FAIR

The Crier in scarlet on horseback

28 Petty Constables on foot

+ + +

+ + +

+ + +

+ + +

+ + +

three drums

banners and streamers

The Grand Marshall

Two trumpets

Town music

x x x

x x x

Two French horns

The Bellman in state on horseback

Four Sergeants at Mace on horseback

* *

The Town Clerk on horseback

The Mayor in robes, his horse led by two redcoats

Two Members of Parliament on horseback

Twelve Aldermen, in robes,

redcoats leading horses of senior men

* * *

* * *

* * *

twentyfour Common Councilmen

+ + +

+ + +

+ + +

+ + +

+ + +

eight Dispensers in their gowns

+ +

+ +

+ +

four Bailiffs in their habits

o o

two Treasurers in their gowns

Gentlemen and tradesmen of the Town

4 Life at the Fair

The day of the opening was like a grander repeat of the setting up, with a longer procession and bigger crowds. Both the town and the University had to make a proclamation, in order to lay down the rules that they were separately going to enforce.

The civic procession left the town with trumpets, music and excited followers, and streamed out to Stourbridge. The parade of gowns and uniforms and the trappings of the horses made a splendid show. They advanced to a ground also alive with flags and music and a welcoming crowd of the Fair-keepers. The smell of roasting goose floated out from the victualling booths and mingled with that from the cheese booths to sharpen everyone's appetite. The Proclamations had to be read in two or three parts of the Fair, but once done, trading could begin, and the officials could disband and make for the special dinners provided in the Mayor's House and the Proctors' Booth.

For the traders, the Fair was a way of life for two to three weeks each year – a working holiday. Once the journey with wagons or carts of stock had been safely accomplished, they off-loaded and arranged their goods. The luxury trades and the victualling booths had to be set up just as if they were moving to a new shop, filling their shelves and stores. On top of that, they had to arrange their beds and domestic stores in the little back bedrooms. The one drawing we have shows a four-posted bed, but an eye-witness talks about small camp beds, that could be pulled out in the morning to air. Booth-keepers and their servants needed to bring their clothes and anything additional for their comfort, as for a camping holiday, but no one tells us about chairs or stools or wash-stands. Cooking equipment was not needed, for the Fair was well supplied with victuallers, providing substantial dinners and plenty to drink.

The main booths were not too uncomfortable, given good weather, but many more traders occupied the 'waste' plots and sites allocated through the Fair, and brought their shelter with them, if they could. Many had tents, but some, no doubt, slept in or under wagons or carts. The smallest traders, pedlars or entertainers, found spaces in the cheapest inns, or in

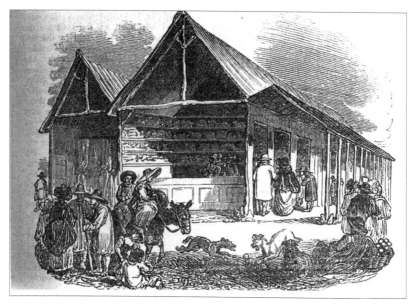

A cut-away view of one of the large booths, from Hone's Year Book of daily recreation and information

outhouses or barns in Barnwell, Chesterton or even further off. They mingled with the poorest of the Fair's customers, and the rag-tag assortment of beggars, petty thieves and prostitutes also hoping to make their way.

One such who caught the attention of the University authorities in 1612, was Thomas King, who had to give an account of himself. He lived, he said, at the Mermaid in Church Lane, in St Andrew's parish in London, and had come to the Fair to meet his brother, who carried cloth from Lancashire for sale. He had stayed Sunday night at Barkway, reached Cambridge on Monday afternoon and stayed at the Cross Keys. On Tuesday night, he slept at a victualling booth at the Fair 'but he knoweth not whose'. On Wednesday, he came into Webster's booth, and spent three hours drinking with a few others. (They were there from 6 o'clock, said Webster.) They left together, but he didn't know them, and then he went to Ditton and lay at the Plough. On Thursday, he was back in the Fair and slept at the Bury Booth, and on Friday, returned to Ditton. The question at issue was his possession of a bundle of fine tagged ribbons, used by gentlemen to fasten and adorn their clothes. Had he stolen them in London? There seemed to be no evidence on the point, and no information about his daytime activities, but he was ordered to leave, to be gone and not come back any more.

The respectable folk who 'kept the Fair', the tradesmen and women, would have hoped to be pretty busy during the daytimes. Selling could start early: Mr Haynes from Holborn who sold linens 'has sold on the first day of the fair 100 pieces of hessens before breakfast'. If their stock sold fast, they might send for further supplies; if sales were slow, they might cry their wares at the door, to draw in more customers, though 'drumming up a crowd' was sometimes a finable offence in the University's eyes. The solo pedlar or entertainer, on the other hand, had to blow his own trumpet. But all took time to renew acquaintance with other booth-holders and regular customers, exchanging a year's worth of news and gossip.

Many came year after year, and counted as old friends. The wool dealers in the 1700s looked out for Mr Savill and his son, from Bocking in Essex, who came every year for over 50 years, and met the wool growers of Rutland and Lincolnshire. Savill noted if any of his regular suppliers were absent. At the far end of Garlic Row in the 1760s was the capacious booth of Mr Green from Limehouse. He dealt in oils and pickles. With him every year came his daughter, whom the undergraduates nicknamed Miss Gherkin or 'Little Pickle'. She must have charmed when she was young, but, as she grew older, she filled out considerably, and her nickname was changed to 'Miss Mango'. She had fine manners, however, and 'it was remarked by an incorrigible punster that she was Wapping in nothing but her size'. Mr Green also attended the fair at King's Lynn (and maybe others?). It's even possible that the Miss S Green, who was attending 40 years later to sell pickles, brushes and soap, was the self-same daughter, grown-up, as well as out and trading for herself.

Many of the Fair-keepers could expect a visit from the University officers inspecting quality, weights and measures. In the eighteenth century, it seems that every seller of alcohol was summoned for 'selling ale/beer/wine/brandy in this fair in measures not sized and sealed by the University'. The penalty was usually a fine of 3s 6d (3s 4d – a sixth of a pound – plus 2d expenses), and most trotted off to the Proctor's Booth to pay up without protest. Some men conserved their dignity by sending their wives or servants to make the payment. It's not clear whether the vessels were brought at the same time, to be checked, or whether the fine was a simple fee to trade, as many customers supposed.

Fines were not always paid up meekly. Occasionally, someone really objected to the court. Stephen Whitlesea, being summoned in 1647, answered back: 'What, should I go along with a company of fools?' Having been hauled along to the court, he continued, 'and used very rude behaviour in putting on his hat and sitting and turning his back on the court when he was upon his examination'. The University was not putting up with that, and detained him 'at pleasure' for contempt. By the next day, he was penitent (or perhaps just sober) and grovelled suitably. He was still fined 5s 6d. In 1612, Thomas Riddman found himself in further trouble when he called Proctor Murriel an extortioner and reviled him. But, according to the record, most of those summoned gave in. The ultimate sanctions were the stocks (at that time, set up outside the Fair court), a whipping or imprisonment.

The owners of gaming tables were also very likely to be summoned before the court. The games aren't described, but are identified as the Roly Poly or the Colour Board. Only one or two raffling booths were fined, though they too were gambles, and a popular diversion. The fines of 3s 6d were too low to deter the proprietors, and the same people came back year after year. In 1725, the commissary, proctors and taxors decided to tackle the persistent offenders. Stephen Jackson was admonished for running a gaming table and told to stop. He didn't, and days later was summoned to the court again. Why had he continued? His answer is not recorded. But next year he was back again, paying his 3s 6d. In all, he (or a relation of the same name?) attended at least 30 years, each one recorded by a court fine.

The proctors' was not the only court at the Fair, for the mayor also had the right to try cases arising there. The Court of Pye Powder (*pieds poudrés* – 'dusty feet') was a medieval institution common to all big fairs, to provide quick justice for people on the move. The mayor's jurisdiction covered cases of theft, debt, breaches of the peace and general wrongdoing. Suspects were apprehended by the Corporation's Redcoats, who roamed the Fair.

Despite the general goodwill and pleasure in the event, rivalries and quarrels, fostered by the plentiful cups of ale, broke out every now and then into assault *vi et armis*. (Even the Corporation liked to record things in Latin, and this tidy phrase 'by force and arms' conceals the sordid detail – unfortunately!) The plaintiff could summon his debtor or assailant to the mayor's court to get instant justice.

 Not many cases came to this length, and it must have been extra shocking when, in 1712, two of the most dignified men in the Corporation appeared in the court. William Watson was a draper, ex-alderman (and probably commissioned the beautiful plaster ceiling in his house on Market Hill) and John Frohock, his accuser, a gentleman, alderman and ex-mayor. Was this some personal grievance, or did it have anything to do with a recently passed Corporation order which prohibited the sale of woollen cloth anywhere but in the Duddery? Watson owned booths scattered in many parts of the Fair, but could only carry out his own drapery business where ordered. Frohock also had many booths, though not in trade himself, including the plum sites at the top of Garlic Row.

The visitors

The Fair drew people from all walks of life, and they flocked in by whatever means they could. The poor walked, others came on horseback, many a man carrying his wife pillion behind him. The most fortunate came by carriage, but every other cart or wagon was used as well. The crowds were such that some of the hackney carriages which plied for hire in London thought it profitable to pursue their trade in Cambridge, running between the town centre and the Fair. The hackney drivers were fiercely competitive, and bawled out their places, seizing on passers-by and all but bundling them into their carriage. For this ride passengers paid 3d. Young couples could pay 1s and enjoy a private ride, with the little tin shutters up to hide from the world. It was a short-lived privacy, as the distance is only 1¾ miles. The Corporation had to deal with the rutted highway that all these wheels produced, and charged the hackney carriages a fee: 2d each trip or 5s for the duration (i.e. the equivalent of 30 trips). The senior bailiff was to collect the money.

Once on the Fairground, interests diverged. In some places, very serious wholesale commodity business was transacted, worth hundreds if not thousands of pounds. Lesser businessmen, such as town and village tradesmen and shopkeepers, sought out discounted goods for resale: cloth, haberdashery, ironmongery and household wares. Stewards and agents, acting for large households, could also command discounted rates on some of the luxuries their employers required, as well as the staples: salt and dried fish, fuel whether wood or coal, soap, cheese. They, too, were stocking up, possibly for a year,.

It was also an occasion for setting aside working clothes and wearing your fair-going best to see, yet also to be seen. A countess, in a party visiting from Wimpole Hall, admired the 'clean countrymen and the maidens tricked out with ribbons and straw hats'. On all sides, people were meeting, hailing acquaintances and friends amidst a general hubbub of salesmen shouting their wares, banging drums or blowing trumpets. For some visitors, like the young people in *The Refusal of the Hand*, the entertainments were the most important thing, and they thronged to the

Maypole

music booth, the shows, the menageries or the theatre (when it was permitted). The young men could raffle for a prize for their girlfriends (or sweethearts, as the term was). Some courting doubtless went on, and some distant glances inspired more than one man to write verses: 'TO THE FAIR UNKNOWN, Upon seeing her in the Music Booth at *Sturbridge* Fair.' Did the poet, Mr Travis, find out who she was? We'll never know.

In the evenings, when the main tide of visitors had ebbed away, the Fair-keepers could shut up their booths – by the simple process of drawing a horse-hair curtain across the door and skewering it with a stick – and retire to one of the many victualling booths. The favourite on Garlic Row

*Style at the Fair
c.1770, tradesman
and lady*

was the Robin Hood. Here, amidst the chat and laughter, the wary discussion of the day's trade and takings, the regulars also met the newcomers, keeping the Fair for the first time perhaps. If both parties hit it off, the regulars would arrange for a Fair initiation ceremony. The eve of the Horse Fair was the favourite time for this rite, conducted with great mock solemnity. It was easily set up, with such props as a college gown, a bell and a chair placed in the centre of the benches.

"Two or three contrive to decoy him, or her, into a sutler's booth, under the pretence of somebody being there to speak with them about business; and then privately send for an old fellow dignified with the Title of Lord Tap, from his going Arm'd all-over with Spiggots and fossets, like a porcupine with his quills, or looking rather like a fowl wrapped up in a pound of Sausages; who when he comes, rings his bell over the head of the Party, repeating these words with an audible voice: [the first verse opposite]

Then the party Christen'd *mandamus* chooses two out of the Company to be his godfathers, who generally give him some very Bawdy name; then they swear him upon the Horns,… make him give the Tap six pence, and spend four or five shillings to treat the company, and then for ever after he's free of Stir-Bitch-Fair."

That was Ned Ward's description in 1700 but, 60 years later, the ceremony still went on. The initiate then had to remove his hat and his shoes and sit in an armchair (much more imposing than a common bench or stool), with 'vergers' carrying staves and candles either side of him. The officiating minister wore a student's cap and gown, and carried a bell in one hand, a book in the other. He began the litany:

'Is this an Infidel?
'Yes.'
'What does he require?'
'To be instructed.'
'Where are the sponsors? Let them stand forward.'
A bowl of punch was provided close to the minister, and he chanted the first four verses.
'Who names this child?'
We do.' And the sponsors provided his new Fair name – Nimble-heels, Stupid Stephen, Tommy Simper – or something else apt or ludicrous. The minister and the initiate each drank the punch, and the verses continued. The 'christening' done, everyone could enjoy a good supper, with plenty of malt liquor, punch and wine.

At night-time, a watch was supposed to be kept at the Fair, as in the town, with Town and University taking turns, and the various colleges all committed to supplying men as required.

Over thy head I ring this bell,
Because thou art an infidel,
And I know thee by thy smell –
With a hoccius poccius mandamus...
Let no vengeance light on him
And so call upon him.

This child was born in the merry month of May,
Clap a pound of butter to his cheek, And it will soon melt away
And if he longs for a sop Let him have ...pray
From his hoccius poccius...

This child's shoes are made of running leather,
He'll run from father and mother the devil[?] knows whither
And here he may run the length of his...
To a hoccius...

This child now to Stirbridge fair is come
He may wish to kiss a pretty wench ere he returns home.
But let him be advised and not to Barnwell roam
For a hoccius...

Nimble-heels henceforward shall be his name,
Which to confess let him feel no shame,
Whether 'fore master, miss or dame ...
With a hoccius

This child having first paid his dues,
Is welcome then to put on his shoes,
And sing a song, or tell a merry tale, as he may choose –
About a hoccius...

"A verse which memory can afford to forget, intervenes before the next"
[Just how bawdy was it?]

Then hand the can unto our jolly friar,
And laugh and sing as we sit round the fire,
And when our wine is out let all to bed retire –
With a hoccius proxius...

Proclamation c.1750

Tenthly That all Merchants and other Persons within this fair Do cease from shewing any of their Wares or Merchandise and from all Labour upon the Lords Day upon pain of such Punishment as by the Law of this Land may be inflicted upon them.

On Sundays, all trade in the Fair stopped for the observation of the Sabbath. From the middle of the sixteenth century, the Chapel no longer functioned, the chaplain dismissed. The little church of St Andrew the Less, back down the Cambridge road, was too small for the Fair-keepers, so the Corporation arranged for a pulpit to be carted to the Duddery, and appointed a preacher to give a sermon. The privilege of appointing the preacher was one of those privileges the Corporation guarded jealously, although they usually appointed a University man of good standing. For the rest of the day, the Fair-keepers were at leisure to wander about, chat and drink as they saw fit. Attending the sermon might be considered a required duty. In the 1590s, an Essex man, questioned later at home about his absence from his parish church, claimed he had been at Stourbridge, and observed the Sabbath there. Another said he had attended St Andrew's in Chesterton.

When their stay was over, traders packed up their tents and goods and loaded their horses and wagons. The carpenters came back to take down the main booths once more and stack the timbers and hair-cloths away for another year. The field had to be clear by Michaelmas, so that the landowners could re-enter it, to plough or to pasture their animals. Anything that remained was theirs to keep, or to plough in as they saw fit. The straw, oyster shells, manure and other rubbish could be ploughed in to compensate them for the tramping down of the ground by the thousands of feet, wheels and hooves.

The journeys home could be as dangerous as those at the outset, but most travelled with a sense of contentment at money made and friendships renewed.

5 *Come Buy!*

Once on the Fairground, visitors would pass naturally to the commodity area that interested them most. Many booths were identified by signs: the Cock, the Woolfleece, the Red Lion, Bagpipes, the Bullshead and many others. (They were not all victualling booths.) The chief business of the Fair was buying and selling, and from its earliest days it attracted a wide variety of commodities and, therefore, a wide variety of customers.

Some areas of the Fair were markets of national significance, as they were chiefly wholesale – the hops, cheese, wool and cloth fell into this category in Defoe's time. Other commodities might be sold wholesale to local shopkeepers, as well as retail to individuals. Medieval monasteries stocked up with food for the winter. The craftsman and the tradesman came for the materials and tools they required, the householder for pots, pans, brooms and baskets. Ladies and gentlemen sought fine materials and accessories for their persons. Few of them recorded their purchases, any more than the merchants recorded their sales, so hard details are few and mostly the result of transgressions. As we know little about the medieval layout of the Fair, we'll follow Defoe's description and the 1725 map to make our tour.

The Fair-goer who arrived from Cambridge in Georgian times was greeted with the aroma of cheese – lots of it. The cheese booths lined the south side of the main road as far as Garlic Row. The booths were smaller than all others in the Fair – a mere six feet wide (less than 2m) – though one seller might have more than one booth. They weren't always spacious enough, and the Corporation tried to insist, by regulation, that the cheeses placed on the ground behind the booths should be removed inside. The Corporation didn't always win, for the late sketch of the Fair shows large round cheeses stacked outside the back of the booths.

The cheeses came from all across the Midlands: Gloucestershire, Warwickshire and Cheshire. An enterprising merchant in 1738, advertised that he would transport cheeses by boat from Thrapston, where he had opened the river navigation, to Stourbridge for the Fair. There were even supplies from North Wiltshire at the end of the eighteenth century, when cheese-making there developed on a commercial scale. The locally-made Fen cheese, from Cottenham particularly, was also sold at the Fair.

The buyers of cheese were both individuals and wholesalers. The cheesemongers, who dealt in London, found the Fair very convenient. For their benefit, the prices per hundredweight were always quoted in the *Cambridge Chronicle*. By Act of Parliament passed in 1563, these wholesalers in butter and cheese were required to obtain a licence from local JPs, which would permit them to trade in these commodities in markets anywhere.

Some of the cheese sellers, challenged by the University officers in 1655–1656 declared they were not really traders, and were merely selling the cheese for their relations and neighbours. Stephen Roberts declared that the four hundredweight (200kg) of cheese he was selling was made by his Aunt 'and that she made it herself and being an Old woman and a widow she imployed him the said Roberts to sell it for her at this Stirbridge fair'. The case against him was thereupon dismissed, but Roberts still had to pay the court expenses! Three Leicestershire men had different tales. One, John Shepherd from Higham, could produce written authority from the makers that they had authorised him to sell for them. Richard Cooper, a fellmonger from Hinkley, said he was factor for a London cheesemonger but he had no way of proving this until, fortunately, the cheesemonger returned from London to confirm it. The third man, Richard Gamble, also from Hinkley, wasn't so lucky. His London cheesemonger couldn't be found, and Gamble was fined.

The quoted cheese prices also provide an index to the rising cost of living in the late eighteenth century. For many ordinary folk, who could afford little meat, cheese was a very large element of their diet. If they could

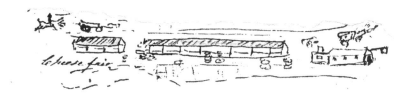

Cheese booths

scrape together enough cash, buying a large stock at Stourbridge made sense. It would certainly be cheaper than buying ounces at a time from their local grocer or the weekly market, and they might even get wholesale prices. This stratagem didn't always work. A plaintive note in the *Cambridge Chronicle* in 1772 alerted readers to a lost sack containing eight cheeses: 'They were bought by a poor Man in the Country, for a Winter's Provision for himself and a large Family.' There were other perils: 'As two men were fighting on Thursday at Stirbich Fair, one of them, named James Seakins, an inhabitant of Barnwell, received so violent a blow on one of his temples, by falling against a pile of cheeses, that he expired in a few minutes.' (*Bury and Norwich Post, 1796*)

The Duddery

Beyond the Cheese Row lay the Duddery, the great cloth market. The King's officers had come to buy cloth for the royal wardrobe in the 1200s, when the Fair was still young and, since then, countless loads and packs had been bought and sold. One of the stories told about the origins of the Fair attributed it to Kendal cloth merchants who, it said, were travelling through the area when, unfortunately, their loads of cloth dropped in the stream as they crossed the Steers Bridge. When they spread them by the road to dry, they made unexpected sales from passers-by, which encouraged them to return the next year, and the next, thus beginning the Fair. As this story was written down 400 years after the beginning of the Fair and makes no mention of the Leper Hospital, it is probably untrue.

When Defoe knew the market, he saw cloth that had come from Halifax, Wakefield, Leeds and Huddersfield, and from Rochdale, Bury and Manchester. Other supplies had come from the West Country and Norwich. Most of the cloth makers remain anonymous, but a few have left a trace. Various Salford and Manchester men brought cloth to the Fair in the 1560s–1580s. Richard Nugent of Salford, linen draper, sold cloth worth £146. His sundry expenses included 2d for 'greasinge my bootes', as well as 13s 4d for his standing in the Fair. In 1643, William Roberts of Marsden paid the same for a place in the Duddery and made a profit of £131 on sales of his cloth. These men brought their wares in horse packs, and Defoe was told there were near a thousand such packs from the North West, unloaded into the vast booths He was told, too, that £100,000 worth of business was done in the Duddery (a suspiciously round figure, that we might translate as 'a huge amount'), but also that much additional business was in orders, with paper transactions.

Woolsack

On the other side of the Newmarket road lay another important wholesale market: the Wool Fair. Swaying wagons brought fleeces in huge bags, called 'pockets', from the East Midlands. That was where the best wool was grown, but it was bound for the cloth-makers (or 'clothiers') of East Anglia. They parcelled it out to the combers and spinsters, who worked in their own homes, and then collected the yarn to go to the weavers, who also worked at home. Towns from Haverhill in the west to Colchester in the east were famous for their manufactures. In Tudor times they brought their cloth to sell at Stourbridge, and had their own rows (Hadleigh Row and the Bury Booths). By the eighteenth century, most of their cloth was exported, but the Fair continued to be the meeting point for the growers and the clothiers. Defoe wrote that the total spent was said to be £50,000–£60,000 – some said more. (A very, *very* rough translation into 2011 values makes that £20m or more.) The Savills of Bocking near Braintree, father and son, came to Stourbridge every year from 1743 to 1817, and the account of their purchases survives. They spent between £500 and £700 a year on wool from Oundle, Corby and Rutland, meeting the same sheep-farmers year after year. Their business finally collapsed when the Peninsular War put an end to their exports to Spain and Portugal.

Close to the Wool Fair were booths selling items of cured leather (the finer quality), particularly gloves for ladies and gentlemen. Gloves were a very popular present, often given to those attending special events, such as weddings and funerals, but also out of friendship, like the four pairs sent to Ralph Josselin's wife in Earl's Colne, Essex, from Mrs Haynes at the Fair in 1658. A little further on was the market for leather and hides, resorted to by saddlers, horse-collar makers and other leather workers. The hides were sold from tents or wagons.

Pressing on towards the river, buyers came to the Timber Fair. The river was a natural route for the transport of timber, particularly imported timber from the Baltic, and in time for more exotic woods from the tropics. Mahogany was popular in the eighteenth century, and was brought into Cambridge for joiners and cabinet-makers. Timber sales were established early on in the history of the Fair, and many gentlemen bought here the wood they needed for rebuilding their handsome houses. Sales continued into the later days of the Fair in the nineteenth century.

Household equipment and furniture

It was possible to furnish and equip a house completely with purchases from the Fair. Between the Timber Fair and Cheapside (the Newmarket road) lay Ironmongers' Row, the pewterers and braziers, the joiners and upholsterers.

From early times, the ironmongery at the Fair was a vital supply, with its own row. In the eighteenth century, the well-known Cambridge ironfounder, William Finch, and his son had a prominent booth here, selling bar-iron. Nails were also vital and had a short row dedicated to their sale.

Other metalware for domestic use was available in Braziers Row. Although named for its sales of brass, pewter became equally important.

Pewter was the fashionable item for every middle-class household in the sixteenth century, and was sometimes bought in large quantities. It was smart enough to display on sideboards, as indicated by the word 'garnish', used to describe an array of a dozen dishes in each of several sizes. But the London Pewterers company grew very protective of their reputation for quality. When they came to Cambridge, they started to object to the local inspection organised by the University, and insisted that only their own inspectors could examine their products. A mighty row broke out over the matter, and the Londoners declared they would avoid the Fair. They were evidently confident that Stourbridge needed them more than they needed Stourbridge. Whatever the outcome of the quarrel (unclear), the Fair survived and so did sales of pewter.

From all the hundreds, or even thousands, of people who bought here, one man's accounts show how you could equip your house. In 1629, the young John Buxton from Mountnessing in Essex, sent his agent, Joseph Valiant, to buy necessaries to set up house with his new bride. Along the Ironmongers and Braziers Rows, Valiant found fire shovels and tongs, dripping pans, a baking pan, two large iron pots, kettles, brass pots, a chafing dish, posnet, ladle, slice and skillets and other bits and pieces. From various joiners and cabinet-makers he purchased three court cupboards, square and round tables and a dozen stools. Then he added two bedsteads, with the rods and cords, a half press (chest) and another table, a close stool and a chair for a child. More tongs and shovels for fireplaces were needed from the braziers, and baskets and mats from the Skip Fair on the other side of Garlic Row. To carry the goods, Valiant paid porters 2d or 3d and another man was paid 1s 4d to load the goods. His purchasing was spread over two days, for he also paid 3s for the load to be watched over for two nights. Valiant's own expenses came to 12s. Altogether, Buxton reckoned Valiant spent at Stourbridge £45 13s 11d, a very substantial sum.

The turners or cabinet-makers were regularly at the Fair. For many years, they fell foul of the University's quality inspectors, for each year they were fined for selling tables 'with sap in the joints'. This may have been a little ritual to preserve the University's rights, for Cambridge joiners took turn and turn about to be the inspectors and the inspected. Thomas, 'an eminent carpenter and joiner' of Cambridge, was fined for over ten years for his sub-standard furniture before he became one of the inspection team in 1738. Once he was off the team, he was fined once more.

The fireplace in the Cambridgee and County Folk Museum with the equipment used in cooking

We don't know exactly what the Cambridge joiners made and sold, but William Tustian, a cabinet-maker from Whitechapel in London, decided in 1768 to advertise in the *Chronicle* and thus provides us with a list of fashionable furniture:

> Cloaths Presses, Desks, Book Cases, Bureaus, Dining Tables, Tea Tables, Tea Chests, Tea Boards, China Trays, Bason Stands, Mahogany and other Chairs, Glasses [i.e. mirrors] of all Sorts, and sundry other Goods of his own manufacture.

How many wagons were needed to bring all that from London? His stock was not quite so comprehensive the next year – perhaps he had learnt from experience what sold best. The year after that, there was a small trade war, for two other cabinet-makers advertised: John Fox from St Ives, and Richard Mathison from Southwark. Fox also sold upholstery and Mathison had a booth next door to a Southwark upholsterer, so they offered this greater convenience to their customers, which Mr Tustian did not.

After this, there are no more advertisements for furniture booths, so we cannot tell if they continued or not. In 1781, Mr Tustian advertised an auction, allocating two days late in the Fair, the 1st and 2nd October, and beginning at the civilised hour of 11 o'clock. The list of goods again provides a vivid picture of the refinements of gentlefolks' houses:

> 'A large quantity of mahogany and other household furniture, consisting of large elegant pier and other looking glasses, in mahogany carved and gilt frames, dressing and other swing glasses, neat mahogany oval tea-trays, ditto tea caddies, ditto tea chests; six neat carved mahogany chairs with hair bottoms and one elbow ditto; mahogany card and other tables; a very fine large ditto; a very good monthly clock, etc. a good four-post bedstead with morine furniture and a curious brass jack with a multiplying wheel.'

Earlier in the Fair's history, it was the mattress makers and feather merchants who were examined closely by the University's inspectors. Some sellers were accused of mixing all sorts of rubbish in with the feathers.

Upholsterers expanded their range of interest as house interiors and furniture became more comfortable. Doolan from Southwark listed his wares for the Fair in 1770:

> 'fine thick Blankets, fine Goose Feather Beds, ready-made Ticks and Ticking in the Piece; great variety of Bed-Quilts, of fine Chintz patterns; beautiful snow white Cotton Counterpanes; Scotch Kidderminster, List, Wilton and rich Persia Carpets; ... also a Variety of ready-made Bed Furniture, of fine Morine; worsted Checks that will preserve their colour in washing ...'

One commodity of particular interest to the University was books. From the Middle Ages there are references to book sales. Some of the London booksellers considered Stourbridge a very useful outlet. There were enough of them to get Cooks Row renamed Booksellers Row. At the Fair around 1700, there were book auctions, and a whole library might be sold thus.

*Book auctions were popular around 1700, but at
Stourbridge were held inside the booths*

In his personal notebooks, Isaac Newton records buying a book on astronomy at the Fair. Ned Ward's account imagines other undergraduates 'liberating' books by slipping them into gown sleeves 'on condition to pay for them if catched'. The booksellers were no quieter in their salesmanship than others at the Fair. Those who auctioned their wares kept up a patter:

'Here's an Old Author for you, Gentlemen, you may Judge his antiquity by the Fashion of his Leather-Jacket; herein is contained for the Benefit of you Scholars, the Knowledge of everything. Gentlemen, I'll put him up at two shillings …'

Later, John 'Maps' Nicholson, famous round the University for his door-to-door selling, kept the Fair:

> Sells books in all Languages, School-Books, Shop Books, Pocket-Books, Writing Paper of all sorts, Pens, Ink, Sealing-Wax, Wafers, Letter Cases and every Kind of Stationery, Wholesale and Retale; with a very great Variety of Maps and Prints as cheap as in London. (*1764*)

Garlic Row

From the booksellers, it was only a step into Garlic Row where the luxury booths stood. (In Elizabethan times, the grocers and mercers were required to sell in Cheapside, that is, Newmarket Road. By 1700, they had shifted.) Here ladies and gentlemen could promenade up and down to see and be seen. The awnings along the front of these booths gave shelter from sun or rain, as needed. Entering the booths was exactly like going into a shop in town, with a counter, stacked shelves and obsequious salesmen.

The grocers' booths were amongst them. The grocers came to the Fair in the Middle Ages with spices, the prized and expensive produce of the East Indies. The very long journey made by cloves, cinnamon, ginger, nutmeg and mace allowed plenty of opportunities for deliberate or accidental contamination with less valuable substances. The University's inspectors did their best to check, but all they could see were the more obvious impurities, and they assessed whether the spices were adequately 'garbelled' or sifted, to remove them. In 1611, for a total of 8 lbs of cloves, 1 lb of middle mace and 4 lbs of lardy mace (in total nearly 6 kilos) 'not well nor sufficiently Garbelled as they ought to have been', John Gibson of London was fined 13s 4d, a large sum for a substantial fraud.

Prices remained high into the eighteenth century. A consortium of Cambridge grocers in 1757 offered cloves and cinnamon at 10d the ounce (28gms), mace at 1s and nutmegs at 7d. Ginger was much cheaper at 6d a pound (454gms) and pepper was from 1s a pound.

With time, the range of goods stocked by grocers grew. Since the Middle Ages, they had sold sugar alongside the spices. Mustard and salt were also sold by grocers, and pickles and vinegar. Let us hope the spices overpowered some of the other savours at the grocers. They also stocked oils, not only for cooking, but also for use as lubricants, fuels and to mix in paints and putty, and so on. Thomas Newling of Bridge Street included in his stock in 1764: 'Oils of all sorts, viz. Barber's, Lamp, Cutler's, Turpentine, Linseed, boil'd ditto'. Washing and laundering materials were also bought from the grocers. They stocked hard and soft soap, powder blue (for whitening linen) and starch.

It was natural that, from the 1660s, grocers' shops should become the outlets for those wonderful new commodities: tea, coffee and chocolate.

Several Cambridge grocers were at one time or other keepers of the Fair. They were in competition with Londoners who came offering all, or part of, the traditional grocer's stock. For at least ten years from 1791, Mr Miller brought teas, coffee, sugar and spices to sell wholesale and retail at No 5 Garlic Row. In his advertisement in the *Chronicle* in 1794, he reports of himself:

> '. . . he has selected several Chests of fine Souchongs and Hysons, etc. from the last East India Co. Sale, of the best flavour and quality … at the following reduced prices, nearly 1s cheaper than can be purchased in the country …'

Tea prices per pound ranged from Fine Green at 3s 6d to Gunpowder at 11s 6d. These prices account for the lockable tea caddies, designed to prevent servants from pilfering this valuable commodity. But the fashion for tea drinking was spreading, despite the cost. It was soon established as a national habit, to the benefit of the grocers.

While the Duddery dealt in woollen cloth wholesale, there were mercers and drapers on Garlic Row to supply lengths in silks, wool or linen for individuals and families. All the accessories of dress were provided as well. There were shoemakers, hosiers, hatters and haberdashers, with milliners displaying a variety of lacy trimmings for ladies. Around 1500, the London silkwomen had brought their fine embroideries and weaving to the Fair. Tomkis wrote in 1607 that so many underpinnings and trimmings were needed for a fashionable lady that 'seven peddlers shops – nay all Sturbridge Fair – will scarce furnish her: a ship is sooner rigged than a gentlewoman made ready'.

The Fair certainly offered plenty of choice. Some of the Cambridge drapers kept booths, but there was competition from Londoners. There were numbers of silk mercers, who were manufacturers in the Spitalfields silk trade or bought direct from the manufacturers, and advertised in the *Chronicle*. Herne and Cox boasted in 1768: 'The Ladies may be assured, as we manufacture our own Silks (and sell for ready Money only) it enables us to serve them on as low Terms as the mercers in Spital-Fields and they may depend on seeing the newest and most genteel Patterns. Elegant Brocades, 23 per cent under their usual price'. From their shop in High Holborn they brought:

a large and very elegant Assortment of MERCERY GOODS ..
Brocades, Tissues, Damasks, Tabbies, Armoseens, Ducapes, Tobines,
Figured Striped and Plain Lustrings, Modes, Sarsnets and Persians,
Thread Sattins ...

The 'Good striped Lustrings' at 3s 3d a yard were a real bargain for ladies
who could afford silk. Cox and Herne did sell cheaper woollen cloth at
prices suited to ordinary folk: 'Callimancoes 9½d. per Yard; Camblets,
8½d. per Yard.'

There was also a growing supply of new ready-made clothing at the Fair
for the trading classes: everything but the finest and most formal outfits
that had to be tailor-made. William Musgrave moved up from Ludgate
Hill in London in 1753 to take over a Cambridge shop on the corner of
Petty Cury, but he also kept a booth at the Fair, in the Duddery. Here he
sold woollen drapery and ready-made clothes. Maybe his first contact with
Cambridge was through the Fair, and this persuaded him that a permanent
move might be advantageous.

The labouring classes had to sew their own clothes at home, or acquire
second-hand clothes. There were second-hand clothes brokers at the Fair,

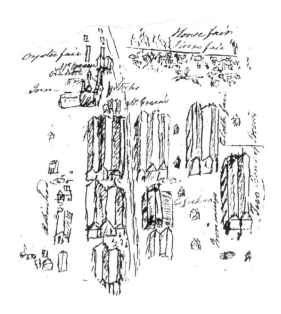

*A view of Garlic Row
drawn late in the life of
the Fair. Mr Green's
grocery booth is named*

in a row near the Common where the other cheaper goods were sold, with stocks of working clothes for labourers. In the village of Fowlmere, vicar, John Crakenthorpe, had to advance his servant his quarter's pay. He recorded that Sam Woods ' wanting his money to buy him some cloaths at Sturbridge Fair, and so had it beforehand, 14s'. The vicar spent nearly twice that on his own black waistcoat, so Sam must have hoped for real bargains at the Fair.

Several traders at the Fair described themselves as milliners/hosiers/hatters/men's mercers, separately, or in some combination.

Cambridge was well supplied with hosiers and shoemakers, but they, too, were in competition at Fair-time with outsiders. The new centre of the eighteenth-century hosiery trade was Nottingham, and several merchants came to the Fair, men like Corneck:

> HOSIER, from Nottingham, and his Warehouse in Cheapside, London With a complete Assortment of Hosiery Goods, Breeches Pieces, etc. cheaper by Five per Cent, than can be bought in London, Wholesale and Retale.
> N.B. And for Encouragement to those who lay out Five Pounds he)allows Discount. *(Cambridge Chronicle, 1764)*

Thomas Smith, shoemaker from London, brought stock with a range of styles, for both men and women, ready-made.

His advertisement on the 22nd September, 1764 begins very confidently:

> HAS opened a booth facing the Coffee Booth in Garlic-Row, with a large Assortment of Boots and Shoes, Men's, Women's, and Children's, both Stuff and Leather, which for Neatness and Goodness of Quality, he desires any Person within Fifty Miles to equal at the following prices...'

Unfortunately for Mr Smith, it would seem that someone did equal his prices. The men's best calf boots, listed at 15s a pair, are reduced in the next week's advertisement to only 13s, and some of his other prices likewise. Men's neat and strong leather shoes at 4s 6d go down to 4s. Women's leather pumps go down from 3s to 2s 9d.

Other dress accessories were supplied by the toymen, also prominent figures on Garlic Row. Toymen were sellers of expensive metalware for adults, rather than for children. Most of their goods were adjuncts or accessories to dress, or more or less personal items: buckles, buttons, brooches and other little things; heads for walking canes, watch cases, tweezers and cases, fittings for dressing tables and desks. (There may, amongst the stock, have been little models in pewter or tin for children to play with, such as toy soldiers or miniature cups and plates, but they are not mentioned.) These luxuries might be in base metals, but could also be in silver, and even jewelled. This was a luxury trade. Of the fop was written:

> He's a mere compound of a toyman's shop,
> Made up of essence bottles, seals and rings,
> Of tooth-picks, snuff-boxes and such gewgaw things,
> His learning dangles in his golden chain,
> Sense, fine as amber, in his clouded cane. *(R Lloyd, 1768)*

From the eighteenth century, large quantities of these luxuries were made in Birmingham, whose metal industries were rapidly expanding and developing. By 1777, there were 129 buttonmakers and 39 bucklemasters, as well as 56 designated toymakers in Birmingham.

Judah Moses' advertisement for the Fair in 1777, lists more of the toyman's stock: silver and plated tankards, candlesticks, coffee-pots, cream-pots 'and all sorts of small plate too tedious to mention', watches 'and great choice of new silver, paste, stone, pinchbeck and plated buckles, and all sorts of jewellery ware . . . '. Of course, these things made ideal gifts, or fairings, for people back home.

With all their clothing needs met, visitors could pass on down the Row to the pottery and china. As with clothes, there were classes of wares, and the finest were in Garlic Row booths.

Of great interest to the fashionable Georgian gentry were the new Staffordshire wares. In that part of the country, several potters were experimenting to produce more refined and decorative wares to supersede the porcelain teacups that were imported with the tea from China. European manufacturers tried to imitate these wares and the result was the creation of china dinner and tea services, replacing pewter and coarser earthenware. Josiah Wedgwood became the most famous of the Staffordshire manufacturers. At the beginning of the eighteenth century, only a tiny proportion of Cambridgeshire homes had any china. By the time Defoe described Stourbridge Fair in the 1720s, there were china warehousemen at the Fair. Around the middle of the century, if not earlier, shops in Cambridge stocked Staffordshire wares. Both Fair and town china-men strove to keep up with the new products. One of Wedgwood's achievements was a refinement of cream-colour ware, which won royal approval and was, in 1765, renamed 'Queen's Ware'. By 1769, William Banks, a potter from Stoke, was selling it under that name at the Fair, 'at his large Booth, next Brittain's Coffee House'. Swinton Pottery near Doncaster, Yorkshire ('Sixty Miles nearer to Hull than any of the Staffordshire works' – was all the pottery being brought by sea?) advertised 'Cream-colour, Tortoiseshell, White-stone earthenware, red Tortoiseshell Dishes, yellow cloudy coarse ware, black commonly called new Colour, and yellow flat Ware'. Sales of china continued at the Fair for the rest of the century, as well as at several china shops in Cambridge. (Not always without problems: when the shelves accidentally collapsed in one Fair booth, £70 worth of china crashed to the ground.)

Glassware was sometimes stocked with china, sometimes on its own. A notable glass man from Norwich, Jonas Philips, kept the Fair at least 14 years until his death in 1770 and was succeeded in the business by his assistant John Cook. They sold both fancy wares for the dining room ('made from the newest patterns now in England'), and functional vessels and phials: 'Surgeons and Dealers, in any of the above Articles, may depend on being served with the best goods on the most favourable terms.' Philips opened sales premises in King's Lynn too, so his stock travelled easily and conveniently by sea and river.

Over to the west of Garlic Row was the Hop Fair. The great heaped bags of hops amazed visitors to the Fair in the eighteenth century, who could not imagine that Cambridge drank so much beer. Hops were unknown to the medieval Fair. Medieval ale was unhopped, and although the plant grew in England from the 1400s at least, it wasn't added to turn ale into bitter beer until Henry VIII's reign. Hence the little rhyme that goes around:

> Turkey, hops Reformation and beer
> Came into England all in one year

which would, if true, have been about 1520. Henry VIII disapproved of this new and strange process in brewing, but it must have caught on, for his law against it was revoked in his son's reign. The way was open for the traditional pint of (warm) English bitter. Hop growing spread in particular areas and, in the east of England, Kent and Essex were chief providers. Stourbridge provided a natural market for sales on to the north. (So Cambridge was not, in fact, consuming all the hops.) In 1657, Ralph Josselin of Earl's Colne in Essex noted that his neighbour hoped to make £500 from his hop sales, though the previous year it had been £790. Josselin does not say what he hoped for his own sales.

Hops were added to the list of commodities subject to the University's quality control, and it wasn't many years before unscrupulous traders were being hauled before the court. In 1611, two Londoners, Ambrose Janning and Stephen Stynes, were accused of selling sub-standard hops, and William Webb was regrating (buying for resale), to make an easy profit.

By the eighteenth century, hopped beer had been improved and its better keeping qualities meant that it could be produced on a larger scale than ale, and sold over an area of several miles. There was less need for households to brew their own, and commercial, or common brewers, as they were called, came into existence in all towns. Hop prices were a matter of great interest, and the newspapers commented on the size and

Hops

quality of the crop. Bad weather ('great rains' and a freak frost in August) put up the price in 1745, but, in 1770, 'Great quantities of hops are expected at the Fair in the ensuing week and from the late considerable crops it is imagined they will be very cheap'. Good cheer for drinkers. Prices were also quoted, and overall they fell during the eighteenth century from around £8 a 'pocket' to £3.

The Skip Fair

Trunks and boxes made of wood were another specialist manufacture with their own row in the Fair. They were sold next to the baskets laid out in the Skip Fair. The baskets came in an even greater range of shapes and sizes. They were made locally, being one of the important products of the Fens. Willows were planted and harvested along all the river banks. Cambridge men negotiated planting rights along the streams within the Borough, but the willow and basketry industry was even greater around Ely.

Water Fair

The parts of the Fair down near the river were called collectively the Water Fair. Here were most of the heavier and bulkier and smellier goods and the more utilitarian products.

While the Fenland baskets were carried to the upper parts of the Fair, the Ely pottery was laid out on the Common, not far from the boats that brought it. Some of the Ely potters advertised their presence at the Fair, but without specifying the nature of their goods – so commonplace as to be unnecessary. These were the jugs, bowls and dishes that all classes used. They were still subject to regulation, and an early version of the Proclamation thundered against the deceitful potters who made vessels too small for standard measures. Maybe that was enough to reform them, so that their gallons, pottles, quarts, pints and half-pints were true measures. If they weren't, it seems that the publicans were the ones to get the blame for selling drinks in short measures. Either way, the potteries survived into the later history of the Fair.

Butter was also very much a Cambridgeshire product. While any country housewife with milking cows could make her own, and take the surplus to sell at her local market, the extensive cattle pastures on the Fens meant there was a large surplus available to send to London. The butter was packed into barrels called firkins, which contained 56lbs (about 25kg) each. Boats carried the firkins from the Fenland farms to Cambridge, where they were offloaded on the Quay and transferred to wagons. Stourbridge Fair provided another important outlet for this trade through the sixteenth and seventeenth centuries. The University took great pains to check quality and quantity, and fined sellers from Wisbech, Upwell, Hemingford Abbots, Fordham and Hargrave in Suffolk, mostly for short weight.

The University's instrument for checking the content of barrels, in its case

Candles were of particular importance to the University, and, whether in town or at the Fair, they were very concerned that there should be a good and sufficient supply of tallow to make them. Most candles were made by successive dippings of prepared wicks in tallow, rendered from cattle or sheep carcases. A better quality candle was made by setting the wick in a mould, and pouring in the tallow. The natural smell of tallow candles was not pleasant, and the very rich preferred wax candles.

The problem for the chandler buying his tallow was to know if the stuff at the bottom of the barrel was as good as that at the top. This was one of the areas checked by the University's inspectors, and they recorded every now and then the villain, such as Bartholomew Gutteridge in 1717, whose barrels 'were found unlawfully packed having a considerable quantity of dross or settlings to mar a third part of the contents'. To find this out, they used a long tube with a section all down one side which was hinged and could be opened. The tube could be plunged the full depth of the barrel, the panel closed and a sample drawn up to check that the lower layers were not rubbish. If there was too much waste at the bottom, the barrels might be confiscated and the seller fined. Oil and soap were also sold in the Fair by the barrel and the same sort of checks were carried out on quality and quantity. When the proctor asked Giles Bridgeman of King's Lynn why he was selling barrels of oil that hadn't been checked, he tried to bluff it out and said they had been checked at Midsummer Fair. He had no evidence though, and was fined 3s 8d and the oil was confiscated.

From the Middle Ages, large quantities of fish were eaten because the Church banned meat-eating on Fridays and other fast days. Fish was acceptable and widely available. Not only was fresh-water fish easily caught, but sea fish could be carried considerable distances inland. In addition, vast quantities were dried or salted to keep longer. Stourbridge had good supplies of all kinds, and many medieval households, particularly the religious houses, stocked up. Newnham Priory in Bedford in one year spent £5 on seven different forms of fish, including ling, salmon, herring and sprats. In later years, the government extended fast days to Wednesday and Saturdays, to develop the fishing industry. (Not because they thought fish was good for people or that meat was bad – they wanted a good supply of fishing boats and fishermen to supplement the royal fleet in time of war.)

Oysters, though strictly seasonal of course, were much cheaper than today and, therefore, more popular. As Stourbridge took place in oyster season, this was the great delicacy of the Fair. The victualling booths were littered with the shells, which were dropped under the tables while the flesh slipped down throats.

Horses

The Horse Fair took place on the traditional Fair date, the 14th September (later the 25th September) and into the twentieth century this was known as 'Ossferday'. There's little or no mention of horse purchases at the Fair in the Middle Ages, but, as the national economy grew, and with it the need for horse-power, the marketing of horses became very significant. These last few days of the Fair each year were vitally important for the horse sales; vitally important, but least recorded. All kinds and degrees of people (as they would have said) needed horses: gentlemen for their carriages and to ride for sport and for travelling, carters, carriers and wagoners to pull their vehicles, farmers to pull their ploughs. Selling horses was a serious business and, because of the value of some of the animals, fraught with perils. They could easily be stolen, and fraud was also a danger. From the 1550s, national law required all horse sales to be carefully documented, and the sales at Stourbridge Fair should have been recorded. Probably they were, but that record has disappeared.

Horse racing became a serious sport in the seventeenth century, encouraged by royalty and, from the 1660s, Newmarket was one of the chief courses, with regular events. But there were many other courses across the country, and the serious interest in betting meant that the regional newspapers, as they came into existence in the 1700s, had many column inches given to listing the runners. Surely some serious sales of pedigree horses also took place at Stourbridge?

The *Chronicle* usually had something to say about sales. In 1769, 'There was a greater number of horses than has been known for a many years past, many of them very good ones which fetched a high price.' There was a similar comment in 1795: 'there was a larger show of horses than remembered for many years. Good ones sold well, but those of inferior sort were cheap.' Seventy years later, the paper asserted 'it is still a good horse fair'. In 1919, when the Fair barely existed, the *Cambridge Press* reported that 'Stourbridge Horse Fair was a little larger than last year. Trade however was very slow indeed.' The next item reported an accident: a boy knocked down by a motor in Mill Road. The arrival of motors was finishing the Horse Fair.

Saddlery and harness had a long history at the Fair, and was one of the few commodities to last well into the nineteenth century, associated of course with the Horse Fair. For seven years from 1790, a London saddler, J Kelly, traded from the Oyster House (or Tiled Booth as he called it). He boasted the patronage of the Prince of Wales and the Duke of York, and his own new designs in horse harness. He was, at first, so enthusiastic about the Fair that he bought the lease of a row of booths at the top of Garlic Row, and let them to a number of drapers and others. He decided to back out of the Fair entirely in 1797, but others continued the harness sales.

The coal heaps

Along the river bank, at the westernmost limit of the Fairground, were the coal heaps. Coal first came to Cambridge in the sixteenth century, when Cambridge men purchased supplies in Newcastle-upon-Tyne. It was called 'sea-coal' because it arrived that way, and to distinguish it from charcoal. A trade developed that combined corn and coal – coal on the boats coming up-river, corn loaded to go out. The Cambridge men involved in this trade were always referred to as 'merchants', no other commodity requiring this general title. The heaps were a feature of the Fair from at least 1561, when referred to as a reference point, to the later days. In the 1820s, the town gas works were established close to this area, to use the coal.

• • •

While there was usually a clear demarcation between buyers and sellers at the Fair, there were times when the buyers came with things to sell. Sometimes they were invited. Mr Philips, the glassware man, asked people to bring their broken flint glass, as he would give a good price for it. A cabinet-maker advertised for supplies of walnut wood. He may have been lucky, as many farms grew a walnut tree or two. Pewter, like glass, could be recycled, and individuals, and institutions like Jesus College, would sell their old pewter back to the pewterers. The churchwardens of Thaxted, like many other churchwardens, required the poor of their parish to work in return for their benefits. They were able then to bring the winnowing fans that had been made to sell at the Fair.

Exceptional times brought exceptional needs. In the religious turmoil of Henry VIII's reign, the parishioners of Great St Mary's in Cambridge agreed to sell the gold chain that had adorned the little statue of St Nicholas with the gold case that held a relic of the Saint at the next Fair. These precious items sold for £2 10s 6d, enough to pay the glazier for mending all the church windows and to buy the quantities of wax needed for candles. The wax could have been bought at the Fair, in cakes bearing the maker's mark, but the churchwardens didn't note where they bought it.

What about the garlic?

Garlic Row seems to have been so named in the Middle Ages, and it seems likely it was named because garlic was sold there. Garlic came from Asia originally and was not grown in the British Isles. From ancient times, it was believed to have valuable medicinal and aphrodisiac uses, so it's very possible it was imported and sold in the early days at the Fair. There are no records to confirm this, no mention of it in all the many and varied lists of commodities bought and sold. The nearest we get to it were the large quantities of onions sold in the Fair in the nineteenth century, long, long after the Row had been named.

We have not discussed all the commodities sold at Stourbridge, but enough is enough, and we might, like the real Fair-goer, need a rest and a cup of something.

6 Food at the Fair

Judging by the number of people fined by the proctors' and taxors' courts, there were around 25 drinking booths across the Fair in the eighteenth century. The fines for selling ale or beer, wine or spirits 'in vessels not sized or sealed by the University', were, by this time, a ritual part of the Fair proceedings. The customers assumed they were being cheated in a modest way by undersized measures, and that the cost of their drink included the fines paid to the University. They also assumed the fines went to fund the University dinner, but didn't let this idea spoil their own pleasure.

While nobody wanted to pay the University 3s 6d (3s 4d, a sixth of a pound, plus 2d costs), the victuallers mostly paid without a fuss. Every now and then someone objected – usually a newcomer and a stranger. Nicholas Alexander came to sell ale at the Fair in 1725, and then disregarded the University summons to the court. The official was sent again, and had the summons on a piece of paper, to give formality to the proceeding. Alexander ripped it up, and tossed the pieces in his face. At that point, ritual stopped and things got serious. Alexander was arrested and taken to the court. He had no option but to pay, and an apology was extracted from him as well.

The University officials were very concerned about their own Fair dinners, but they weren't too concerned at this time about the food served up for others to eat, as long as it was 'wholesome for man's body'. There were several kitchens attached to booths in different parts of the Fair, though one lane in the Fair was designated Cooks Row (or by Ned Ward 'their Greasinesses Division') where most cooking was done. The Cambridge cooks, Peter and John Betson, had booths there in the eighteenth century. A hundred years earlier, religion played a part in the menu, as eating meat on Fridays was not allowed. The proctors fined a number of people for offering meat for sale on Fridays in the Fair.

It's not clear if the large quantity of bread that was needed (everybody's staple food) was baked at the Fair, but, if not, presumably the bakers of Cambridge and Chesterton got up even earlier than usual, to bake extra.

The Sewster family, who owned and leased booths in Garlic Row, were bakers, but the University officials fined them for selling alcohol in measures 'not sized or sealed'. Wherever baked, the bread was subject to the current price and weight regulations, and the Commissary's court dealt with any baker trying to take advantage of the situation.

The smells of fish, cheese and roasted goose drifting across the Fair encouraged everyone to turn to the victualling booths. The early morning had seen suppliers of the meat, bread and other essentials calling round the Fair. By mid-morning, there was roasting and baking aplenty for the Fair-keepers and the visitors. While there were many pedlars selling fruit and walnuts to stay the appetite, dinner was an important part of the day.

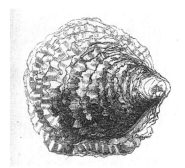

Oyster shell

Oysters were the great delicacy and eaten in vast quantity. They formed part of the formal feasts of the University and the Corporation, and they were slipped down in booths across the Fair. The larger variety – as big as a horse's hoof – came from King's Lynn, the small from Colchester. An observer noted that the shells were tossed under the tables, and a deep litter formed that never left the site. Shells are still found in modern times and, of course, have given the name to the present-day Oyster Row.

The finest victualling booths, such as the Coffee Booth, advertised accommodation suitable for ladies and gentlemen.

In 1768, a joker from the country decided for a bit of fun to order a dinner at one of the booths 'for a [fictitious] large company' who would arrive at 1 o'clock. At another booth, he ordered two geese to be prepared for a 2 o'clock dinner. Then he trotted along to the Coffee Booth, to dine and the Favour will be gratefully acknowledged, by their humble Servant,   JOSEPH KING.

JACOB BRITTAN, at the TUNS Coffee-House, begs Leave to inform the Nobility, Ladies, and Gentlemen, that he intends keeping a COFFEE-BOOTH at STIRBITCH FAIR, as usual, which will be fitted up for the Reception of Company, in a much more commodious and genteel Manner than last Year; to consist of two Rooms, one for Coffee and Tea only, and the other for the Entertainment of Gentlemen, &c. at Dinner. The Nobility, Gentlemen, &c. who shall please to confer their Favours, may depend on the best and genteelest Accommodation, and the strictest Attention to give Satisfaction.——The London Papers every Day.

N. B. Great Care will be had to make the Rooms warm and convenient.

☞ There will be always a good Larder, and Dinners dress'd at the shortest Notice.

WANTED immediately, an Apprentice to an Apothecary and Surgeon. Any Gentleman

Cambridge Chronicle, September 12th, 1767

alone, but couldn't resist boasting of his trick. The man, who overheard him, told the victims, who fetched the Redcoats, who made sure he paid up. The crowd that had gathered thought that was the best part of the joke, and 'the Humourist left the Fair directly and has not since been heard of'.

Both Town and Gown officials and their guests had special dinners, after they had formally proclaimed the Fair. The mayor's party included the Members of Parliament (Cambridge had two) and country gentlemen, and was held upstairs in his brick booth. The bailiffs had to supply the dinner out of the money they had collected in tolls and rents. As these things do, the provision tended to get out of hand, and every few years there was some regulation to prevent abuses and cut back costs. At one time, diners were sending some of the dishes down to their servants, hanging round hungrily outside. The Corporation laid down a careful set of rules to deal with the problem. At the end of the meal, the senior sergeant was to have two dishes from each course, then the bailiff making the dinner was to set the remains before the sergeants and gentlemen's servants in a decent manner, after taking some out for the Redcoats. If there was anything left after that, the bailiff could decide what to do with it. Unappetising as it must have been by then, there were probably people glad to have the scraps of roast meat and puddings. Some years later, it was the wine that was disappearing from both the mayor's booth and dinners in the Guildhall, 'a practice so mean and scandalous' that guilty parties were threatened with a fine of £20.

Meanwhile, the University party also did well for itself. Henry Gunning, later the University Registrar, remembered the customs that were used in the 1780s. Despite plenty of cakes and wine before they left the Senate House, the company was ready for dinner straight after the Proclamation. At this date, they assembled in the Oyster House on Garlic Row, although they had to force their way through the drinkers in the public bar on the ground floor. Upstairs, the party of 30 to 40 squeezed into a partitioned space at one end and enjoyed barrels of oysters with ale and bottled beer. When that was done, they left the building to walk up and down Garlic Row a few times, while waiters reset the table with a cloth and the main course: two large dishes each of herrings, roast neck of pork, plum-pudding, boiled leg of pork, pease pudding, goose, apple-pie and a round of beef. The dishes were cold by the time they reassembled, but that was accepted as part of the occasion. The dinner and toasts with 'execrable' wine lasted the afternoon, until it was time to go to the theatre.

Victualler

7 Entertainment

After business came pleasure. The entertainments at the Fair were the best that Cambridge folk were going to see from one year's end to the next, and the crowds at the Fair encouraged some of the smartest touring shows and exhibitions to come and try their fortune. Defoe lists 'puppet-shows, drolls, rope-dancers and such like; of which there is no want'. The other commentators of his time are no more forthcoming with detail, so the information we have comes chiefly from the University court records, and from the newspapers. The University's concern in this context was to fine Fair-keepers for gathering a crowd, 'contrary to the proclamation'. Fines did not deter showmen any more than they did the other traders.

The variety was greater than Defoe implies: single animals (exotic or deformed), menageries, clockwork models, human 'freaks', as well as music and variety shows and, from the mid-eighteenth century at least, live theatre.

Every deformation in an animal, or oddity of growth in a human being, could be exploited for gain. A succession of dwarfs and giants displayed their statures at the Fair. Some announced their own coming through the *Chronicle*:

> 'We are desired by Mr Henry Blaker, the GIANT, to assure all lovers of Natural Curiosity, that he will be at the ensuing Stirbridge-Fair, there to exhibit himself to the Publick, where he hopes he shall give a general Satisfaction, as he has already at London, the University of Oxford and at Bristol.' *(1751)*

Some travelled far: Maria Theresa, the Corsican Fairy, came in 1771, to be seen at Mr Bullman's booth from ten in the morning until nine at night. 'She is 28 years of age, only 34" (86cm) high and weighs but 26 pounds (16.8kg).' The usual entry charges applied: ladies and gentlemen 1s servants, etc. 6d. In 1781, Margaret Morgan, 'the Monmouthshire fairy', got a bigger billing in the *Chronicle*'s editorial matter. She was 'an amazing sight … her astonishing littleness, admirable symmetry and pleasing spriteliness' had already delighted the King and Queen the previous month at Windsor. 'This amazing part of the human species is now in the 24th year of her age, and not 18lbs (8.2kg) in weight. Her form affords a pleasing surprize, whilst her admirable symmetry engages the attention; and for the inspection of the curious she will continue at a commodious booth, joining Mr Brewer's Coffee-booth in Garlick Row.'

Taking advantage of the Fair visitors in 1753, the young giant from Munster, Cornelius MacCragh, was to be seen at the Wrestlers, in Petty Cury, during the time of the Fair. Aged 16, the boy had reached a height of 7 feet 4½ inches (2.25m), it was claimed.

The Female Colossus came in 1764, 'who for her stupendous Height and just Symmetry and Proportion of Body, is allowed to be the tallest and finest Woman in Europe'. She was to be seen daily, from 8am to 8pm, at James Bullman's, adjoining to the Shew Booth. 'Prices, Gentlemen and Ladies according to their Liberality, tradesmen, etc. 6d, Children and Servants 3d.' Was there a gentleman mean enough to stoop to pretend to be a tradesman? Did some tradesmen like to assume the status of gentleman?

1784 promised both Mr O'Burne (the noted and most wonderfully astonishing IRISH GIANT), and Miss Hawtin (the Coventry Young Lady born without arms):

'This curious artist threads her needle well,
And does the wonders of the age excel;
She with her toes exhibits more to view
Than hundreds with their fingers ever do,
That hundreds flock to see her everyday,
And all improved go satisfied away.

Admittance to ladies and gentlemen 1s'

Animals were presented as scientific curiosities, to encourage gentlemen from the University and others of a serious mind to inspect them. In 1723, there was a tiger, in 1725, an ostrich and in 1741, Stephen Gauden brought a rhinoceros. From then on, wild creatures were regularly advertised until in 1797, there was competition between the Exeter Change menagerie from the Strand in London (*just arrived in four large*

broad-wheeled magnificent caravans') and 'The LARGEST EXHIBITION OF
FOREIGN ANIMALS in this Kingdom, now in the possession of Wm
Cross lately from the Tower of London'. Each promised an elephant, and
a tiger, as well as other amazing delights. Mr Pidcock of Exeter Change
spent more on newspaper advertising (he took nearly 10 column-inches
in the *Chronicle*), but maybe he had to counter malevolent rumours. A
news item in the same edition ran: 'Information that a Tiger broke out in
the Menageries at Exeter-change, Strand is totally without foundation.'

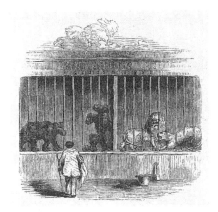

Menagerie

In 1748, the Thaumasticon (or Double Cow: a Greek title encouraged
those who claimed learning: thauma = marvel, mastos = breast) had
various parts of its anatomy duplicated on its back, including a second
udder 'which UDDER as well as the Natural One gives a large Quantity
of Milk'. Mr John Pinchbeck was fined 3s 6d for gathering a crowd to see
the animal, but the newspaper promised that 'several Gentlemen of the
Royal Society and great Numbers of the College of Physicians ... have
seen it, think it the most uncommon and extraordinary curiosity they ever
saw or read of alive'.

More fun were the learned animals. Learned pigs or dogs (even a horse)
were trained to pick out, or identify, letters from an alphabet in order to
'answer' questions put by their trainers. This was immense fun for some
of the undergraduates who fed the showman with pieces of local, or even
University gossip. He would then cast his questions to make the animal
reveal embarrassing, or hilarious, answers implicating local celebrities –
good fun all round. The '*Chien Savant*' turned up in 1751, ('Note. He reads,

The Wonderful Pig was sketched by Rowlandson early in its career, two years before it reached Stourbridge

Writes and casts Accounts by the means of Typographical Cards.') and the first of the learned pigs arrived at the Fair in 1785. He outdid the dog, as he 'solves questions in the four rules of arithmetic, tells, by looking at any gentleman's watch in the company, what is the hour and minute, in short he is the admiration of all who have seen him'.

Another, more dignified, amusement was the exhibition or waxwork show. The proprietors would present the most up-to-date events, or popular heroes, in their displays. Resounding British victories, such as Admiral Duncan's over the Dutch fleet (1797), or natural events, such as the eruption of Vesuvius in 1794, were a good draw. The waxworks did well with figures of royalty, and Mrs Sylvester's collection of 1794 perhaps excelled everything that had gone before. She had modelled both the English and the late French royal families, prominent politicians and even John Wesley. The figures were made 'by that Eminent Artist Mr Sylvester, late pupil of the Royal Academy of Paris. They are all richly dressed after the newest and most splendid taste of their respective countries'. The show was open from 10am to 10 in the evening and, while Ladies and

Gentlemen were charged 1s each, there was the usual reduction for Tradespeople, Servants, etc. – 6d. The most curious exhibit was 'A most Beautiful Sleeping Venus, Full length, lying on a bed, being the most exact imitation of Nature ever seen': artistic, no doubt, but far too lifelike for some people. Mrs Sylvester was brought before the Cambridge court charged with exposing to public view a wax figure of a naked woman. She was fined £10 (or 400 tradesmens' admissions) 'which she immediately paid' – and probably laughed all the way to the bank.

Earlier in the century, Henry Bridges of Waltham Abbey had designed and built a clockwork machine some 10 feet (3m) high with clocks and astronomical panels, panoramic scenes and music. He called it the Microcosm, and it seems one of its early outings was to Stourbridge in 1735. The gentlemen of the University would have been fascinated by its planetariums and model of Jupiter and moons, but the officers of the court still fined Mr Bridges for his 'show'. (It returned to Cambridge to the Falcon Inn in 1752, and to the Fair in 1772.)

Christopher Pinchbeck, Snr. was also a clockmaker, who developed musical automata which were displayed at fairs. One of these was perhaps the 'Universal Theatre of the World', shown at Stourbridge (and fined) in 1730. In 1731, he brought a Musical Clock (as did other showmen over the years). His sons continued his line and, in 1742, built the Panopticon. It apparently didn't reach Stourbridge until 1751, but was worth the wait. It consisted of a tall structure, 'a Triangular Musical Machine with six moving pictures, which is universally allowed, from its beautiful structure, the variety of its Motions, and the Harmony of its music, to be the first Piece of Mechanism of its Magnitude in Europe'. The clockwork in the interior worked figures in the six scenes, which were a concert at a country fair, a shipbuilding yard, a founders' shop, a smithy, a stonemason's yard, and a landscape with mills working, carriages passing and a dog duck-hunting. Once in the booth, the visitor could walk round and round the Panopticon, marvelling at the myriad moving figures and machines busily going about their business. Cambridge people were assured that 'This beautiful Piece of Mechanism has given the greatest Pleasure and Satisfaction to most of the Royal Family, Nobility and Gentry of London'. No doubt the Commissary felt a similar pleasure in fining Mr Pinchbeck for gathering a crowd.

The Microcosm and the Panopticon played music as part of their performance, and music in any form was popular at the Fair. There seems always to have been a music booth on Garlic Row. Mr Hill, the Latin writer of 1702, describes the little crowd at the door, enjoying the music for free. The door was kept by a jester or clown, called in those days a Merry Andrew ('paltry jokes of a Merry-Andrew upon his stage'): 'before the doors he stands gloriously attired in motley Cap and dress to vie with painted flowers. He pretends stupidity, and rejoices to be thought a jest. Leaning on an Oaken Staff ... his hard face bursts into great Whinnies of excited Laughter.' But not always. In 1722, the University court recorded that Sam Hardy, door-keeper to the Music Booth, was accused of 'striking the [Proctor] Bowyer Sneyd in the said Music Booth on Tuesday 11 September at about 7 o'clock at night'. Hardy, the Merry Andrew, was to be restrained (which could have meant a night in the Tolbooth lock-up), but, fortunately, his employer, James Miles, proprietor of the Booth, appeared and guaranteed his good behaviour. Hardy was released with Mr Sneyd's consent 'he having asked pardon of Mr Sneyd and paid the court fees'.

James Miles was the proprietor of the Entertainment Gardens at Sadler's Wells, just north of London, from 1699 to 1724. For at least seven of those years he also ran the Music Booth at Stourbridge, paying the University annually 11s for the privilege, as he also sold wine there. It must have been a pleasant place to sit then, after trawling up and down through the Fair. We have no idea what music was offered by Mr Miles: popular airs perhaps, or pieces of Purcell, Handel or overseas composers? The indefatigable Ned Ward described the Sadler's Wells Musick House in 1699:

> *The organs and fiddles were scraping and humming,*
> *The guests for more ale on the tables were drumming;*
> *Whilst others, ill-bred, lolling over their mugs,*
> *Were laughing and toying with their fans and their jugs*
> *Disdain'd to be slaves to perfection, or graces,*
> *Sat puffing tobacco in their mistresses' faces.'*

Let's hope better manners prevailed in Cambridge.

In 1767, rival music booths were set up. They each promised 'A GRAND CONCERT of Vocal and Instrumental MUSIC', but Goodhall's booth further advertised *The Beggar's Opera* (one of the hits of 1728) and *The Citizen*. Further up Garlic Row the Sussex Band was presenting *The Busybody* and an entertainment called *The King and the Miller of Mansfield*. In 1774, the *Chronicle* announced there would be 'a spacious Music Booth erected, and Grand concerts performed every day, the Vocal parts by an exceeding good Company selected from London, Dublin, Edinburgh, York and Norwich'.

As the variety shows at Sadler's Wells grew more elaborate, so did the entertainments sent up the road to Cambridge. By eschewing drama, they kept clear of the licensing rules that applied to plays and players. In the 1740s, the Company was run by Mr Rayner and, in 1745, advertised 'the usual diversions':

> Rope Dancing, Tumbling, Postures, singing, Balancing, and variety of Stage-Dancing, both serious and comic; particularly by the celebrated Miss Rayner, who for Truth and Height of Dancing, is allowed by all to be the greatest Performer now extant. To conclude with several new Pieces, in Grotesque Characters, call'd HARLEQUIN'S MASQUERADE, etc.

By the SADLERS WELLS Company.
At a commodious Booth, the Upper End of
GARLICK ROW, Stirbitch, the Public will be en-
tertained with a Variety of Performances; particularly,
STIFF ROPE DANCING.
By Mrs Baker, Mr Lawrence, and Mis Baker,
Several curious Equilibres on the
SLACK WIRE.
By Mr Lawrence,
GROUND and LOFTY TUMBLING.
By the Polander and Mr Baker.
Together with SINGING, DANCING, &c.
To which will be added, a Pantomime called,
HARLEQUIN RESTORED.
Boxes, 2s 6d Pit, 2s First Gall. 1s Upper Gall. 6d
Different Performances every Night.

Cambridge Chronicle, 1768

Mr Rayner 'doubts not of giving satisfaction'. Prices were: boxes 2s, Pit 1s, Galleries 6d – 'to begin every day at Two o'clock and end at nine'. It seems that the provinces were being given the same variety and quality offered to London audiences. The Harlequinade was a popular introduction from Italy and the forerunner of the pantomime.

(In 1765, a proper theatre had been built at Sadler's Wells, with prices at 2s 6d, 1s in the pit and 6d gallery.)

As a substitute for live theatre, puppet shows were very popular. There were a number of regular venues in London, and more shows toured the provinces. Some used glove puppets, the forerunners of Punch and Judy (and Mr Punch often appeared, although his wife was called Joan), but there were also stringed marionettes of varying sizes. The standard was 45 to 60cm high, allowing the possibility of plenty of movement and crowd scenes, but later in the eighteenth century, larger wax figures were used. The showmen promised lifelike movements, as well as splendid appearance, but it is impossible now to say exactly how this was achieved. A variety of plays, scenes and tableaux were shown, although the perennial favourite was the *Creation of the World* (including Bible stories up to Dives and Lazarus, concluding with vista scenes of heaven and hell). Elaborate backdrops and scene changes were an important part of the show and sure to please.

The puppet shows thrived, despite being the occasion of one of the greatest tragedies Cambridgeshire had ever known. A certain Richard Shepherd stopped with his family-run show at Burwell on September 8th 1727, surely on his way to Stourbridge just 15 km (8 miles) away. He hired a barn and stable for the night and, with wife, daughter and two servants, set up his puppet show in the barn. The opportunity for the villagers was enticing – for 1d they could see a show on their doorsteps without walking to the Fair. Some 140 people packed into the barn. They enjoyed the preliminary performances – conjuring by a performer who stood on a table in front of the set (the table was then folded up and put out of the way across the barn door), and a two-handed piece by the Shepherds. But earlier, an ostler employed by the barn-owner, coming to his work in the adjacent stable, had hoped to be admitted free to the show. Told he must pay his penny, he had retired, but found a chance to climb over the partition between stable and barn. As he scrambled over straw bales, the candle he was carrying lit the straw, and the flames roared up to the timber roof. In panic, the audience fought for the barn door – barred by the table and also inward-opening. Eighty people died in the crush and the fire. Many of them were identified in the casualty list as 'son', 'daughter' or 'servant', so were probably children or teenagers. It was a terrible loss for the Fen village.

Mᵣˢ BRITTLE the beauty of TUNBRIDGE WELLS
This proves what oft you've heard and oft you'll find,
The face is sure the index of the MIND.

All fashionable resorts had a raffling shop, and that at Tunbridge Wells was kept by the formidable Mrs Brittle. Maybe William Vincent, at Stourbridge, was a jollier person!

At the Fair, games of chance were a great lure. Several booths offered gambles on the roly-poly board or the colour board. There was also at least one raffling booth, where young gentlemen could hope to win an attractive prize for their young ladies. It was conducted rather differently from a modern raffle:

> Full in the midst of all the Fair there stands
> A booth adorned by more than common hands
> A Raffling booth tis called by men below
> The Nymphs Delight, by gods that better know,
> Where each puts in his shilling for a throw.
> The nymphs surround you with impatient eyes,

Hang o'er the box and flutter round the dice
And then if the propitious fates ordain
That You fling highest and the Raffle gain,
The lady's smiling sweetly o'er and o'er.
For various fancies there are various things-
Some Girls love China, some delight in Rings

The Refusal of the Hand, anon

The heroine in this burlesque poem has so flouted polite convention that she has no one to buy a ticket for her, and mopes about the Fair alone, until the time comes to go to the theatre, where she is put to even greater humiliation by her erstwhile friends.

They were lucky to have a performance to go to. Of all the travelling showmen, players seem to have been the most suspect to the authorities. Often considered little more than wandering vagabonds, they depended in early times on the patronage and support of an influential nobleman, or even royalty. Numbers of these companies had come to Cambridge and performed for the Corporation since the Middle Ages. In 1642, the theatres were closed completely by Parliament, on account of their pernicious influence. Presumably Stourbridge Fair was likewise without plays or interludes. In 1660, at the Restoration of Charles II (the 'Merry Monarch'), London theatres reopened and there was once more a theatrical world to spread out into the provinces. Now it was enlivened by the addition of actresses to the public stages, where only men had played before.

In Cambridge, the University still maintained the right to approve or ban public entertainments, and the players kept up a running tussle to get approval. There is no reference to theatre at the Fair before 1670, so we can only speculate about earlier companies evading the University officers.

The eighteenth century opened with a notable incident: the famous actor Thomas Doggett (best known later for founding a race for the Thames watermen) brought a company of actors to Stourbridge. As the subsequent court cases reveal, he had contracted with the mayor of the town, William Newling, a carpenter, to build a theatre booth and to provide the necessary permission for Doggett's company to perform. At the cost of £40, the Theatre was to measure 70 feet by 32 feet (20m by 10m, not the only edifice of this size in the Fair), and Doggett oversaw the building and fitting up. He said he had approached the Vice Chancellor for approval of the list of the plays he proposed to put on, but was brushed aside. Optimistically hoping all would be well, the Company took the stage. But all was not well. The Vice Chancellor had no intention of allowing any plays, and the University took action, appointing an additional 62 graduates as supplementary proctors to patrol the Fair. The proctor and his officers went to the theatre, where *Hamlet* had begun, and hauled the actors off the stage. They were imprisoned at the direction of the Vice Chancellor for at least 12 hours, and Doggett was required to sign a bond for £500, payable if he tried to act at the Fair in future. This rather high-handed reaction was the responsibility of Dr Richard Bentley, very recently appointed Master of Trinity College and thence (by a process of turns round the college heads) the new Vice Chancellor. He wanted to establish his authority right away, and Doggett provided the opportunity.

In 1737, a particularly biting satire performed on the London stage led to the passing of the Licensing Act, which required all plays to be approved by the Lord Chamberlain before performance. Meanwhile, it seems actors had been performing at the Fair, and Mr Joseph Kettle had decided to build a permanent theatre. He intended, he said, to entertain people coming to the Fair:

> Plays and Interludes have for many years past been constantly acted during the Time of Sturbridge Fair within the Town and precincts of Cambridge and the same having been Acted in a Number of Common Wooden Booths and Boarded Places to the great Hazard and Inconveniency of the Spectators [Kettle has] for the regular and Convenient performing of Plays during the Time of Sturbridge Fair only, at his own great and sole Expense Erected and Built a Commodious and Convenient Playhouse in the Precincts of the Town of Cambridge upon his own Land for the Entertainment of the Company who should come to Sturbridge Fair and in which Plays were performed during the time of the last Fair in a much more orderly decent and Convenient manner than had been before usually done.

The University objected. Mr Kettle's petition to Parliament was rejected, and the Universities of Oxford and Cambridge had their own Bill approved, which declared

> That all Persons whatsoever who shall for Gain in any Playhouse, Booth or otherwise, exhibit any Stage Play, Interlude, Shew, Opera, or other theatrical or dramatical Performance, or act any Part or assist therein [within 5 miles of Oxford or Cambridge] shall be deemed Rogues and Vagabonds ...

with the possibility of being locked up and put to hard labour for a month.

But within a few years, the fortunes of the theatre at the Fair changed. The University lost interest in prohibition. Perhaps some of its own members wanted the chance to enjoy the theatre at home. Certainly, by the 1790s there was a keen band of supporters led by the Master of Emmanuel College, Dr Richard Farmer, and nicknamed 'the Shakespeare Gang'. One small ironic note: in 1772 Steven's company played *The West Indian*, a popular play written by Richard Cumberland, grandson of that Dr Bentley who locked up Doggett in 1701. In 1779, there were two theatre companies and a show from Sadler's Wells, advertised with much detail about the performers and the treats to be offered.

For many years, the Norwich Company came every year, making a stop at Stourbridge part of their East Anglian tour. They presented a variety of playwrights, from Shakespeare to the newest London production. Their manager for 11 years, John Brunton, also commended his Company

Theatre and show booths

to audiences by giving benefit performances whose proceeds went to the charity schools of Cambridge and to the relief of prisoners for debt in Cambridge Castle.

Towards the end of the century, the newest spectacle was the equestrian show of Mr Astley, which boasted the feats of young Master Astley, as well as troops of others, combining horsemanship and gymnastic tricks.

There were many other delights advertised down the years, and Fair-goers could make their way home well amazed, instructed and entertained.

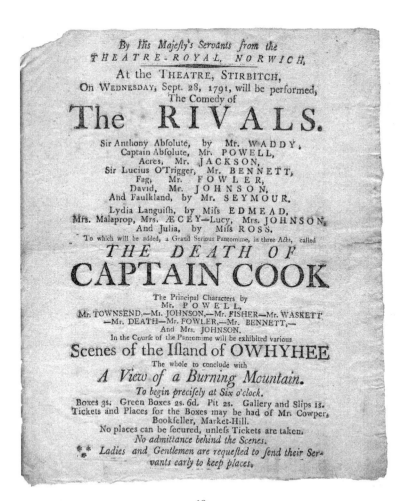

8 Trials and Tribulations

The excitement and anticipation of the visit to Stourbridge was always tinged with worry. There were the dangers of the road, and the possible attentions of thieves and tricksters to add a *frisson* of fear to the happier thoughts. Defoe himself, in his other writings, imagined the pickpockets, thieves and whores of London following the merchants and the hackney cabs up the road to Cambridge to see what pickings were to be had. Ned Ward suspected the students themselves were not above stealing books, if they could get away with it.

Every class of society had reason to worry. In 1763, a poor man, who had been working at the Fair, was on his way home down Maids Causeway when he was robbed of 9d – paltry takings, but still enough to buy bread and ale. On the other hand, a gentleman lost over £40 from his stolen pocket-book. Some losses cast light on the commercial networks of the time. Before banks were universal, to save carrying cash, many businessmen gave hand-written bills, like cheques, that their creditor could cash from a third party, acting as banker. In 1765, such a bill for £60 was lost between the Fair and Earith. It had been drawn by a man from Diss, Norfolk, to be paid by a London company. The finder was asked to take it to either of those men, or to an individual in Wainfleet, Lincolnshire, or to another in Earith.

Means of travel to the Fair varied, but all had their risks. For those who could afford to ride, a horse could bring problems. Mr Harwood, peruque-maker of Ely, riding with his wife seated pillion behind him, was on his way when the horse fell, throwing them both. Mrs Harwood suffered a broken leg and her husband was much bruised – a very sorry end to their trip before they had even reached the Fair. Some travellers were unlucky, some tempted fate. Wagons and carts were generally stable, if not very comfortable, if you sat in them. The dare-devil lads who decided to ride on the shafts beside the horse could easily slip and fall under the hooves and the wheels, and the papers reported many fatalities.

The most alarming (or maybe exciting) hazard was the highwayman. The 'Gentlemen of the Road' were rife on the main roads outside London in the eighteenth century. The wise traveller gave in to their demands and suffered no physical hurt, but every now and then a combative spirit resisted. In 1770, Mr Davidson, a seedsman of Upper Thames Street in London, fell in with another traveller (as he thought) on his way to Stourbridge. In a narrow lane, his companion turned on him, demanding his bank note, cash (42 guineas) and his watch. Davidson demurred over the watch, and a tussle ensued, the highwayman using the weighted end of his whip as a cosh, and then pulling out a knife. Davidson fought back and, ultimately proving both stronger and luckier, he was able to snatch back his possessions and gain the safely of the turnpike house. The *Chronicle* does not report whether the highwayman was caught.

A more subtle villain pretended to be a brother Quaker when he fell in with Zachariah Whyat riding from Saffron Walden to the Fair. Whyat was taken in, and confided that he had a hard-earned 50 guineas in his pocket. At this, the highwayman revealed his true colours and demanded the money. Whyat returned that he would have to work for it and flung the purse with the money over the hedge. The highwayman leapt from his horse to find it, giving Whyat the chance to jump from his own very poor nag and ride off on the highwayman's much better horse. At least he had the chance to recoup some of his loss.

Booth-keepers needed to bring their clothes and creature comforts for an extended stay, but travelling with both stock and household was perilous. Not too surprisingly, things were lost. One unfortunate owner in 1745 could get no news of her box, and was reduced to advertising in the *Cambridge Journal*:

> 'Lost last week between LONDON and STURBRIDGE FAIR   A Middle-siz'd deal box   mark'd on the Top IO' and containing three fine lady's dresses, one in brown damask, one in a pink silk and 'a new-fashion'd flower'd Cotton, with six shifts, seven pair of sleeves, eight night-caps, and three pair of cotton stockings, with some aprons and other small things. ...'

Poor Mrs IO was evidently expecting to enjoy a fine time at the Fair and must have been distraught. Finders ('no questions asked') were desired to contact John Oswald, bookseller from the Poultry in London or the newspaper proprietor in Cambridge.

The Proclamation of the Fair included this instruction:

> Also we charge and command that all common women and misbehaving people avoid and withdraw themselves out of this Fair and precincts of the same immediately after this cry, that the King's subjects may be more quiet and good rule may be the better maintained.

The stated penalty was imprisonment, but the stocks or the pillory could be used and some offenders were whipped. On the other hand, the majority of offences dealt with by the Pye Powder Court seem to have been settled with fines. They included fights and arguments about merchandise, with incidental defamation. ('He has been in most of the gaols in London.' 'You are a rascally cheating rogue.')

The more professional villains were quite good at evading capture. Pickpockets were always about, for there could, indeed, be rich pickings. In 1795, a gentleman from Suffolk lost his pocket-book containing £30 to £40 which the thief took, but also £400 in drafts (cheques) which he didn't. These were found in the pocket-book, thrown behind a booth. Another gentleman had his pocket picked of £12 while he was going into the theatre. Numbers of other people had purses stolen, with the culprits escaping detection. Some losses were not on the Fairground, but in lodgings, which were often shared. A man staying at the Blue Boar, in the middle of Cambridge, was robbed of £41, while he slept, by the man in the second bed. A few years earlier, a pickpocket was collared by his victim, and his name (Robinson) and details, were sent off to Bow Street. Presumably he looked as if he might have 'form'. (Interestingly, these details were all published in the Bury St Edmunds papers, but not in the *Cambridge Chronicle*. The Cambridge editors were clearly intent on protecting the reputation of the Fair.)

Although a night watch was kept at the Fair, and the Redcoats were about in the day, tradesmen had to keep watch over their stock for there were few ways of securing it. Even the timber booths had only cloth doors. The most common hazard was simple shoplifting, especially of small items of dress or haberdashery – handkerchiefs (worth stealing, when they sold for 3s), ruffles, small capes, and so on. Goods on wagons were also vulnerable, like the load of 38 horse hides that was lifted from a wagon standing overnight on the Common near the Chapel. A guinea reward was offered for the return. It might be the seller that was at fault, as in the report of a lost leather parcel to be sent to Robert Spellman, a horse-collar maker at Bury St Edmunds. Livestock could be more vulnerable. In 1770, 'on Thursday last', a person dressed as a dealer mounted a horse to try him and then rode full gallop up Garlic Row. Fortunately, the owner realised the trick and raised a pursuit which scared off the thief, who abandoned the horse and escaped in the crowd. On another occasion, Joseph Pendridge of Fen Stanton tried to steal a black mare from Mr Green of Bolnhurst of Bedfordshire, but he was caught and committed to the Castle gaol.

A different sort of catastrophe befell an exhibitor of animals when his ostrich died. The loss of so distinctive an exhibit must have been a blow, albeit an inevitable one. However, the death provided an opportunity to dissect the bird, and the paper reported the interesting collection of ironware and coins found in its gizzard.

Amongst the hazards (as they deemed it) of attending the Fair, and one which both Town and Gown tried to control, was the influx of prostitutes. The University considered itself responsible for the students' morals, as most of them were minors, and college Fellows were also bound to celibacy. Whatever the senior members' conduct (and no one ever supposed them entirely innocent), they had to make a stand against prostitution and always presumed it was the girls who seduced the students, and not the other way about. The officers were particularly agitated in 1611 at rumours flying round. The Fair book noted:

> Platt of Cambridge deposeth upon his oath that two or three
> days ago he heard at Richard Hulls the Butchers
> that there was a Londoner he thinketh they said his
> name was Clappam that had brought 55 or 56
> Wenches to the fair and that he had hired the
> Timbers booth and that he paid 50s for it ...

On the next page, the clerk added in letters an inch high **'Hugh Clappam, he was taken last night in Barnwell'** and added in normal script that there was only one maidservant, but anyway they had locked Clappam up in the Tollbooth (gaol). Two other women, apparently without husbands or regular lodgings, were hustled out of the Fair instead. Panic over.

Ned Ward gleefully assumed that the students took the opportunities the Fair offered to the meet the girls who came down from Lynn, even though they might rue the consequences later. It was said the Lynn women remained on the barges, which became floating brothels. The hamlet of Barnwell, between the town and the Fair, always had a reputation for brothels, being both poor and distant from the proctors' patrols. The *Chronicle* reported how one Barnwell girl, nicknamed the Limping Chicken, had spent the night with an Oxfordshire wool dealer, but made off early in the morning with his watch and 25 guineas. The dealer pursued her, coach stage by coach stage as far as Downham, where he caught up with her. He brought her back to a Cambridge inn, 'where after some little parleying' he took back his watch and most of his money and let her go. She was lucky in her customer – if he had turned her in to the law, she could have hanged.

All you wanton wenches	*What happened unto you*
Which in Venus delight	*I hope you remember*
A little come listen	*When you were at Sturbridge faire*
What I shall recite:	*In last September:*
And let this same Dittie,	*Where you had store of such*
Cause you to beware:	*Vilde whipping cheare:*
How that you come any more	*As that I think, you will sing*
At Sturbridge faire	*Come no more there*

Street Ballad c.1625 from Pepys Ballads, Pepys Library

The weather, usually kind to the Fair, was not always so. A very wet summer could flood the Common, and rain during the Fair could penetrate the canvas and haircloth shelters. High winds were even worse. A violent storm swept over the Fens on September 8th 1741, laying flat many of the Stourbridge booths 'in one of which a poor woman who has kept the Fair upwards of 70 years and is 102 Years of Age, lay then a dying by the bruises she received' reported the *Ipswich Journal*. In 1772, a storm struck on Friday 25th September, after the *Cambridge Chronicle* had gone to press with details of the theatre programmes. Undaunted, Mr Hodson prepared a second edition to inform readers: 'This morning by the violence of the wind, which was more terrible and dreadful than has been known here for many years Mr Bailey's large Music Booth at Stirbitch Fair was blown down entirely to the ground and many other booths a good deal shattered'.

The worst calamity for many was when there was no Fair at all. Six times in the seventeenth century – 1625, 1630, 1636 and 1637, and 1665 and 1666 – the Fair was cancelled by royal proclamation because of serious outbreaks of plague in London or Cambridge. Outbreaks of plague had been known since the Middle Ages and there were many others, as well as flu and smallpox epidemics, but officialdom usually left people to decide whether they wanted to take the risk of mingling with unknown folk who could be infectious. There were times when notices had to be put in the press to affirm that there were no (longer) cases of smallpox in Barnwell or Chesterton. Fortunately, although no one realised it at the time, the 1665–1666 outbreak of plague was to be the last substantial occurrence in England, and that was the last time Stourbridge Fair was prohibited.

'Amongst the various accidents produced by the high wind this week at Stirbitch fair, the following may be considered as the most tragical: a lady walking on the road with a gentleman, who had long paid court to her, a blast took her in the front, and entirely unroofed her of her hat, cap, tow, horse-hair, and French curls, and left her as bare as if she had been new shaved: the lady burst into tears at so dreadful a discovery, and the gentleman, after picking up the shipwreck of her beauties, stood motionless like a statue, with all the head-furniture in his hand, and so mortified at her appearance, that he had not power to give her comfort by a single word.'

Cambridge Chronicle, 28th September, 1770

75

9 Owning Booths

For centuries, the Fair was agreed to be a great asset to Cambridge, but in what was it most important? Certainly, everyone enjoyed the society and the entertainments, but these were really the icing on the cake. The substance was in the money brought in. No one doubted that there were handsome profits, and Queen Elizabeth's charter of 1589 had been very explicit about it, yet Cambridge never looked like a wealthy town and, by the eighteenth century, it was considered quite mean and shabby. Horace Walpole commented in 1763: 'the town is tumbling about their ears'.

It's clear that the income generated was spread about. Since many of the traders came from other parts of the country, they took their profits with them. Their contributions to the Cambridge economy came in other forms. For a start, as Defoe pointed out, traders and customers between them occupied all the available accommodation in and around the town. The poorer folk sheltered in barns and outhouses. We can assume innkeepers upped their prices, and the two or three weeks of the Fair earned a disproportionate share of their year's income from rooms, food and stabling. There were a few individual beneficiaries, like the ferryman at Chesterton – the ferry to Stourbridge Common was little needed at other times, but was continually busy in September, as there was no bridge between the Great Bridge in town and that at Waterbeach. Many other poor folk in Cambridge and Barnwell earned themselves pennies for portering, watering horses and other small services.

Owning a booth, or booths, was one way of making money from the Fair. There were profits in booth-ownership, although calculating them can be difficult. By the time of Nutting's survey in 1711, around 66 people owned booths or leased them from the Corporation, only about a third of the town's freemen. Sir John Cotton was the biggest holder, with booth frontages totalling 428 feet (140m). At the other extreme, Mr Robson had a single booth of 12 feet length (less than 3m). Sir John's successor collected £68 annually in rent from his Fair booths. We know from the later accounts of Miss Tryce Mary Parratt that her three booths earned £21 a year, but substantial sums went to carpenters and suppliers when the booths were put up, and to the Corporation in tax. The expenses varied year by year: at the lowest £9 17s 2d, at their highest £16 18s 7d. So the annual profit might be only £4 1s 5d, but could be over £11.

How anyone came to own a site in the Fair in its earliest days is completely unknown. In the way of these things, it seems likely that traders who returned year after year established a traditional right to a particular position. It was the custom in medieval towns for like trades to gather together, and this was probably an early influence – the principle was certainly applied in the Fair for a long time. Once the Cambridge Corporation took over running the Fair, it was established that only Cambridge freemen (burgesses), could own booths and booth-grounds along the principal streets in the Fair. They could then use the booths themselves, or let them to the many traders who came from elsewhere to sell at the Fair.

There was no suggestion that every freeman should be entitled to a booth, so the inequalities we have just seen probably arose quite early in the Fair's history. To keep control of the situation, the Corporation insisted that any transfers of booths, whether by inheritance or sale, had to be conducted before the mayor and at least one alderman. The Corporation ordinances were all recorded in the Cross Book, a compendium that was regularly consulted down the centuries, whenever the Corporation wanted to check how things had been done 'in times past'.

The transfer of booths was regularly entered in the Common Day Book, a record of the Corporation's meetings or 'Common Days'. Death or retirement were the usual reasons for transfer, but sometimes there were sales, as owners lost interest, or changed their business, or moved away. But not every man, who moved out of the town, wanted to sever his personal or business links, and some were determined to hang on to their booths. The Corporation was worried that this might drain away the active participation from town residents, so they instituted hefty penalties. Some booth-owners were paying £3 a year to keep hold of their booths, while they lived in London, or Chelmsford, or even Surrey.

The Corporation also kept some booths in its own hands, the treasury booths, which it let out. Over time, it became responsible for more booths, as owners decided to devote them to religious and charitable purposes. Before the religious changes of the sixteenth century, many a man or widow, making a last will, would make provision for a priest to say regular masses after their death, sometimes for years, to help release their soul from purgatory. A small property needed be set aside to provide the fund to pay the priest – what better than Stourbridge booths? The requisite booths were officially returned to the Corporation, which would lease them out and pay to have the masses said. Sometimes it was a condition that the Corporation officers attend these services, and often there was to be a handout of bread to all the poor folk who attended to add their prayers. The booths were recorded in Corporation ledgers by the name of the last owner: Helgay, or Kent, for example.

After the Reformation, in the Protestant Church of England, there was no purgatory and no masses. All the resources dedicated to this end were officially confiscated by the Crown. The royal Exchequer grudgingly released the sums that had been left for the benefit of the poor – just over £7 was reckoned to derive from the booths. Yet the booths themselves somehow remained with the Corporation. The idea of commemorating a life by good works did not go away. Henceforth, donors gave booths to pay for annual sermons, to exhort and instruct Cambridge folk, preached in one of the parish churches. There was still often an accompanying dole of bread for the poor. In this indirect way, a little share of the proceeds of the Fair reached the poorest in the community.

The treasurers' accounts which list the Corporation's income survive for some years, but not all, and the details are not always clear for the modern reader. Estimating the Corporation income from booths is, therefore, rather approximate. However, it seems that in 1561, the Corporation was receiving nearly £46 in rents from its Fair booths. This did not go up with even the modest inflation of the next century, and a hundred years later the total was about £50. In the eighteenth century, the amounts set down are the same, but the accounts end by exempting more and more of the debts. By 1789, virtually no money was being collected.

In 1711, when Howland Nutting had his survey of booth ownerships carried out, about 14% of the booths were in Corporation hands. If we assume the Corporation's share of the booths was representative of the total of booths (and some were clearly more valuable than others), the potential rent income for all the booths was about £350. This would be a substantial sum, yet it bears no comparison with the turnovers that Defoe suggests the traders were enjoying. Perhaps the private owners managed to get more out of their tenants, while the Fair was flourishing. Those who traded in their own booths may have done better yet.

The regular transfers of booths to relations accounted for most changes of ownership and draw a picture of family relationships down the years. We have already seen how the Nuttings' booths crossed the generations, and other families showed similar histories. The parties, or their representatives, had to come to the Guildhall for the formalities, for in law the booths were being surrendered to the Corporation, and thence awarded to the new owners. If the new owner was not a freeman of the Borough, he had first to be made free, and then he could be admitted to possession of the booths.

Although women could not be freemen, they could be treated as if they were, as in the case of Elizabeth Howland. A daughter could inherit booths from her father and, while she remained single, enjoy the use in the same ways as a freeman. If she married, by law all her property became her husband's. Although a husband became the lawful owner, he could not dispose of his wife's booths without her consent. If he wished

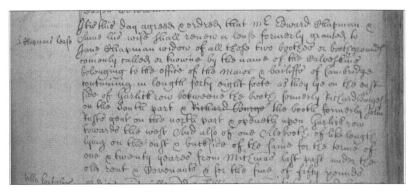

Extract from the Cambridge Corporation's Common Day Book, recording renewal of the Chapmans' lease of The Calveskins booth, 1689, in the Cambridgeshire Archives

to sell her booths, his wife was questioned separately at the Guildhall, to confirm that she agreed to the sale. Widows regularly inherited their husband's booths (although more commonly they passed to children). If the husband had leased booths from the Corporation, his widow was allowed to carry on the lease.

This was the situation when the daughters of William Welbore, draper of Cambridge, deceased, came to the Guildhall in 1660 to claim his booths. The first step was to make their husbands freemen. One was John Ellis, a former college Fellow and now vicar of Waddesdon in Buckinghamshire; the other Samuel Newton, a notary living in Cambridge. Ellis then had to pay a regular fine because he was not a resident. Despite this geographical separation and very different fortunes, the two families stayed in touch and, in his last will, Sam Newton remembered his nephew John Ellis, then living in Westminster, in disposing of his booths and other property. Newton also bought some booths from Christopher Bumstead, a pewterer. (But why did a pewterer, who could trade in his booths, sell them to a professional who saw them rather as an investment?) At his death, Newton left his booths in Cheapside and the Duddery to his son John for life and thereafter to John Ellis, six booths on the west side of Garlic Row to son John and his heirs, and four booths on the east of Garlic Row to the Corporation.

A booth lease could descend through many generations of one family. Alderman Edward Chapman renewed his lease of a booth timber house on the main road in 1661 and died in 1668, leaving his widow to take over. Their son, also Edward, a woollen draper, took the lease in 1689, with his wife, Anne. He died in 1695 and again, Anne (as his widow) took over the lease until their son (a third Edward) could succeed in a joint

---

Key (selected) to 1820s plan of the Fair as it was c.1770
A small ancient chapel, B little inn (is this or R the Oyster House?), C shows, D theatre, E Cheese Fair, F Wool Fair, G Hop Fair, K Suttling booths, L little edifices of general convenience, 1 – 5 luxury goods on Garlic Row, P Ironmongers' Row, Q Coffee House (kept by Dockerell of Cambridge), T Horse Fair, W Coal Fair, X clothing for farm workers, Y Hatters Row

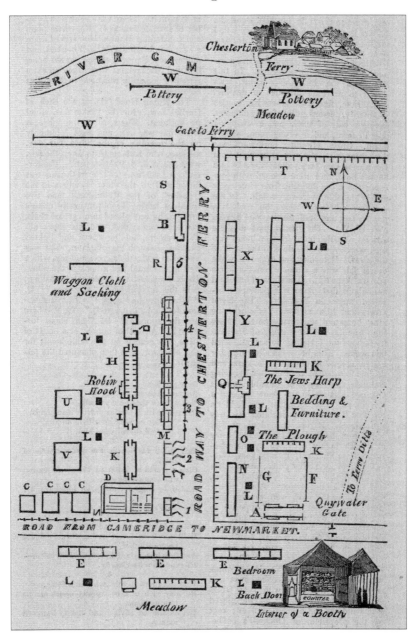

Plan of the Fair: remembered c.1820

tenancy with his wife Sarah. She took on the lease jointly with her brother, Edmund Halfhyde, a Fellow of St Catharine's College (a rare case of a member of the University holding booths). Fifty years later, the same booth was still leased by Chapmans.

When John Sewster, a baker from Holy Trinity parish, died in 1721, he provided in his will that his son, Elias, should inherit his booths on the west side of Garlic Row, known by the sign of the King's Arms, and his daughter, Mary, should inherit the booths he leased from the Corporation on the east side of Garlic Row (the ones given to the Corporation by Alderman Newton). His wife, Alice, had been running one booth as a victualling booth, selling ale and wine, and she continued to do this until 1724. (Like the other victuallers, she had to pay the University a fine each year for using vessels that hadn't been approved.) Elias, too, was fined by the University, until 1751 (and including 1748, when he was the mayor). In 1779, another Mrs Sewster advertised for sale one of the booths, a victualling booth called The Queen's Arms, but there was still Stourbridge Fair property for Mary Sewster to leave to her daughters in 1783. As late as 1810, one of them, Jane, left her share to her sisters. Maybe the Sewster property was still of interest because it lay on Garlic Row. By 1800, the Fair had shrunk drastically, and scarcely extended beyond the Row.

Sometimes the transfer of booths makes it possible to trace the fortunes of a family. Francis Percy was a stone carver who came from Devon to work in Cambridge. He was employed in various works round the colleges – the shield over Clare College door, 'great heads, capitals and festoons' and work on the Wren Library at Trinity College. He became a freeman in 1687, nominated by the mayor, and himself became mayor in 1709. He acquired three booths and intended at first to leave them to his three daughters. At his death, however, son, Charles, a milliner, and daughters, Elizabeth (married to Dr Perkins), and Margaret (married to Mr Trevor), each received one booth. Charles' booth descended to his son, who became a student at Corpus Christi College and then a clergyman. His daughter, and then her young daughter, Tryce Mary Parratt, had inherited the three Percy booths by 1763. The accounts that we have already looked at were saved with her husband's family papers (the Baumgarten archive) and are still in the Cambridgeshire Archives.

10 The Decline of the Fair

When Defoe wrote his wonderful account of the Fair in his Tour, he implied that his visit took place in 1722. A look at the dates shows this was not so. He was relying on what he knew from earlier visits, maybe dating back to his younger days in trade as a hosier. His was already a historic view. The book had been in circulation only a couple of years when the Nutting brothers inherited their late father's booths and booth grounds. Going through the formalities in the Council in 1726, Howland Nutting, Jnr. was moved to object to the entry fines and rents he was being asked to pay. The booths, he said, were much lessened in value 'by reason of the Decay of Trade'. The Corporation agreed, and allowed him £20 off.

The two Nuttings' surveys – Howland, Snr's of 1711 and mayor Thomas's of 1725 – do highlight some changes, most notably in the Duddery. The great enclosure described by Defoe is, indeed, complete in 1711, the listed booths forming a whole rectangle. But in 1725, the fine new map shows no booths at all along the eastern and south-eastern end, a loss of 245 feet of frontage. Nevertheless, no one else renewing leases made this objection to their rents. What was going on? A temporary blip? Special pleading for Howland Nutting? There is no other complaint about any lessening of trade at this point. The other evidence all indicates confidence in the Fair. Heirs to booths and booth grounds were apparently keen to take them up. The hackney coaches were still so busy conveying Fair-goers up and down the Newmarket road that they caused serious damage to the road and annoyance to the Corporation.

The next published account of the Fair was in a general survey of Cambridge made in 1748–9 and published in 1753. The writer, Edmund Carter, describes the Fair much as Defoe did, using his very words in many parts. He sees no reason to change the lists of goods and entertainments provided. The only changes he mentions are tiny: the maypole that once stood in the Duddery is no longer put up. The youths who tag on to the mayoral procession are no longer given cakes at the end of the proceedings.

It is in a summary of the town's financial affairs that Carter demonstrates what maybe he thinks is self-evident: the value of the Fair has diminished. The land-tax that the Corporation had to pay to the Crown used to include a contribution of £256 19s 10d from the proceeds of the Fair, he says. (This was what the bailiffs were collecting when they allocated spaces in the open areas of the Fair, and collected tolls.) In 1729, there had been a change in the arrangements. In that year, the senior bailiff, King Whittred, had offered to pay the Corporation a flat sum of £120 in return for the right to collect and keep the tolls of the market and Midsummer and Stourbridge Fairs. The arrangement continued. By 1749, says Carter, only £112 7s 10d was raised from the Fair 'that being very much declined of late years'. A decline in toll income of over 50% is, indeed, substantial. It does not necessarily mean that the volume of trade had declined by the same proportion, but that is the implication.

From about this period, local newspapers are published, and provide their evidence of commercial affairs. They contain announcements that certain Cambridge tradesmen are giving up the Fair. These men can, they feel, offer the same service in the greater comfort of their permanent premises and, by promising 'Fair prices', they 'doubt not of giving satisfaction'. In 1745, Mr Jordan, the ironmonger from opposite Trinity College, declined keeping the Fair. Two years later, Thomas Cheetham the draper, did likewise. In 1757, there was a greater stay-at-home movement, in which four grocers agreed together to sell from their shops only, and advertised jointly with a list of commodities and prices. Susan Powell, the milliner, did the same, so did Henry Darwent who sold Manchester Ware (drapery) from his warehouse in Free School Lane. It is from about this period that we find shopkeepers generally giving more attention to the display of their goods and the comfort of their customers. Shopping, for the well-to-do, became a pleasurable leisure experience, to be enjoyed more frequently.

National and international changes in commerce and trade were also gathering pace, and their pace was ultimately in the wrong direction, literally and figuratively, for Stourbridge. At first, the new areas of production – Yorkshire, Lancashire and the West Midlands, did supply the Fair, and copiously, as we have seen. But there were even greater markets to supply, largely overseas in the new colonies and the trading areas in Asia. The goods needed first to go west, to Bristol and the emerging port of Liverpool. The home market was also growing in all these new areas, and decreasing in rural East Anglia.

Another factor was the change in domestic travel. The improvements in major roads made by turnpiking (collecting tolls to fund better road repairs) were cutting journey times across the country and producing smoother rides for gentlefolk, who might more readily go to London, or, indeed, expect a better and year-round supply of London goods in their local markets. By 1776, there were two or three fast coaches making the journey from Cambridge to London well within a day (though the fare was high – about the same as a week's wage for a working man). All these reasons for the decline of the Fair were listed by Caraccioli in his *Historical Account of Sturbridge, Bury and the most Famous Fairs* [etc.] in 1773. He thought Sturbridge had been declining for 20 years.

The *Cambridge Chronicle* was, however, aware that the Fair was still very important to Cambridge businessmen. Even if they were not at the Fair, they needed the extra visitors to keep coming to their shops. The *Chronicle* did what it could. On September 13th 1764, the editors, Fletcher and Hodson, announced 'We have the pleasure to inform our Readers of the promising appearance of Stirbitch this year; a greater number of booths are already built, than have been seen for many years past. The Shew Booth is much larger than usual, and we are told that a Company from Sadlers Wells are coming down to perform in it during the Fair.' And they would not print anything that might put visitors off: 'The humorous description of Sturbridge Fair abounds with too many indecencies to have a place'. Four years later they were delighted to report that 'the trade in general at Stirbitch this year has been much more considerable than last, and it having been exceeding fine weather for this week past, more Company have resorted thither than for several years before'.

However, by this time, the Corporation was losing interest in the Fair. Increasingly, booth lessees were being excused their rents, and the general income from tolls on goods continued to be farmed out. The processions and dinners continued till the end of the century, but they had more to do with local politics and relations with local gentlemen and members of parliament. The fact that the Corporation was a trustee for the charitable use of revenues from booths was forgotten. What profits there were disappeared into private hands.

In the 1790s, times became very hard for the humbler folk who made up the majority of the population. Food prices were rising, while wages remained more or less constant. Bad harvests in the mid-90s led to catastrophic rises in bread prices and major unrest. A potential riot in Cambridge was quelled when the mayor, John Mortlock, seized grain from the mills and distributed it free. Ordinary folk had little spare money for fair-going, and the better-off were facing the first levies of income tax.

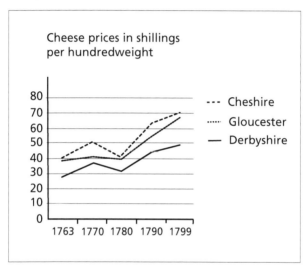

1802 was a really bad year. The Mayor's Booth was taken down in January. For a while, the theatres had provided an attraction that encouraged Fair-goers, but this season a disastrous stampede was caused by false cries of 'Fire!', which left four people dead and many injured. This prompted the building of a permanent theatre nearer town. Shows were put on there at the same time of year, September to October, with the same varied programmes, and theatregoers did not need to go out to the Fairground.

Despite this, the Fair kept going, although a shadow of its former self. There were fewer takers for booths and the Fair had shrunk back to Garlic Row and the Common. The Horse Fair, held on the original Fair day, now

September 25th, became the most important feature, with sales of saddlery and leather goods, timber, onions, and smaller supplies of hops and cheese, taking place over a week or less. The luxury commodities – the silks and fine china, the silver and glass – disappeared. There were still drinking and show booths, although the entertainments were not of the national class, as in the past.

There was also a serious threat to the old Chapel, for it was no longer used to store booth materials and was too far away to be a valuable pub booth. Fortunately, an academic, Thomas Kerrich, who realised its historic importance, bought it in 1816 in order to preserve and restore it.

Along Newmarket Road, brickpits and kilns were being developed to supply the building boom in east Cambridge. Gradually these spread across land formerly occupied by the Fair.

The decline continued. The *Independent Press* said in 1837: 'This once celebrated mart is every year falling off in its importance'. The *Chronicle* observed that most sales were retail, rather than wholesale, as they used to be. The tradition of celebrating at Fair-time was still observed, although far fewer people actually went there. In 1846, diarist Josiah Chater, an apprentice bookkeeper to Eaden Lilley at his store in Market Street, noted of Fair Day: 'We have had an extraordinary day of business, both in saddles and other wholesale customers. Have not been so busy for a long time …. it has been a very good fair, but goods were dear.' Next year: '… and busy we were all day long. I did not leave the counting house till ten o'clock, which is late now as I generally leave on Saturdays by nine. It has been the finest fair day since I have been here.' Many folk still got an extra special dinner on Horse Fair Day: 'The men dined in the yard off a piece of beef and pudding according to the general rule.' At Mr Ingle's house (a currier at 24 Market Street) 'We had a good lunch of a wonderful piece of beef which, when whole weighed 80lb 9oz (36.6kg), the like of which they make it a rule to have every Stirbitch fair.'

When Josiah and his brother were ready to set up their own drapery shop in 1850, they set off by train on the 9th September to go to Huddersfield, Leeds, Manchester and London to buy their stock. It arrived in Cambridge in time for them to open their shop in Sidney Street on the 24th

September – ready for the additional business that Fair Day brought to the town. How very different a picture from earlier times! The railway they travelled on cut across the land that had once boasted the huge Duddery sales.

The Oyster House in 1864

There seems to be no record of what happened to the semi-permanent timber houses along the Newmarket road, but Mr Alpha's House in Garlic Row survived. It was called the Old Oyster House – a memory, probably, of its life as a victualling booth, and the University dinners held there. It is listed in Spalding's Directory of 1874, on its own with no occupier or neighbours. In 1919, it had a caretaker, Henry Brown, and by 1922, 18 houses had been built beside it, running up to the Newmarket road. Henry Brown now lived in an adjacent house, as a gardener.

All over England, the Victorians closed ancient fairs because they had become troublesome haunts of drinking and crime (or so the middle classes thought). Despite Mr Young's petition mentioned below, it would seem that Stourbridge was not greatly troubled with these problems. After its reform under the Municipal Corporations Act of 1836, the

25th Being Horse Fair day I was on Special duty from 9 AM until 3 AM on the 26th same duty from 12 noon to 1 AM. A Donkey & Harnes & one sack of Onions was Stolen from the Fair last night.

Journal of Elijah Larkin, policeman, 1857

Corporation still exercised its privilege of collecting tolls and dues, and determined the times of operation; yet, although the Fair was now of only minor local significance, it could not bring itself to close it down. By 1871, Stourbridge Fair lasted only three days, and offered swingboats, coconut shies and roundabouts alongside a few sales of onions, cheese, hops and household utensils.

After the First World War, the Fair's death knell was finally sounded with the collapse of horse sales. The petrol engine was now driving carriages

Joseph Romilly, University Registrary:

"September 1850

Th 26. Horrid wet day – rain from morning till night. – Court at 'the Great Tiled Booth' Stirbridge Fair: no Proctor attended & only one Taxor ... exactly the same number of cases as last year, viz 16, whereby I gained £1. We walked home by the river so I missed making my customary purchase of gingerbread in the Fair: I however bought the same quantity in the Town.'

September 1857

Mon 27 Mr Young's object was to get my signature to a memorial of Cambridge Householders concerning the immorality of midsummer and Sturbridge Fairs. He wishes the 'tippling and dancing booths' to be put under more surveillance of the Police, and also that ten o'clock should be the hour for closing. He says these booths are positive brothels and that they have a room separated by a curtain. ..I signed it.

Romilly's Cambridge Diary, 1848–64

and farm machinery, and few needed horses or their harnesses. Only a handful of people came to hear the Fair proclaimed and to buy gingerbread or ice-cream. In 1933, Stourbridge Fair was proclaimed for the last time, by the mayor, Florence Keynes. On the 5th July 1934, the Borough issued the official notice, signed by the Home Secretary, to abolish the Fair.

The Oyster House survived longer, although neglected. It was occupied some of the time, and a young academic lived there with his family in 1951, with undergraduates going there for supervisions. The house was finally demolished in 1957 and Oyster Row occupies the site.

Leper Chapel interior

The Chapel had a mixed career. Having organised its restoration, Kerrich gave it to the University to preserve. Two more episodes of restoration were needed in the nineteenth century, in between which the Chapel was used for services for the navvies building the railway in 1845, and then for the brickfield workers and finally for a first World War Military hospital (a return to its beginnings). Maintaining the Chapel is a burden, and the University repaired it one more time before handing it over to the

Cambridge Preservation Society (now Cambridge Past Present and Future). Occasional services became regular, under the auspices of Holy Cross Church. The Preservation Society and the Friends of the Leper Chapel organised a continuing programme of events. In 2004, a little 'Stourbridge Fair' was organised for Saturday 11th September to commemorate its great predecessor. It continues annually (to date), a tribute to one of the most important institutions of Cambridge's past.

The modern celebration of Stourbridge Fair at the Leper Chapel

Appendix: Visiting traders at Stourbridge Fair 1745–1802

This list is a partial one only, compiled from two main sources:

1. The account written in 1820 by a man who attended the Fair in his youth, from 1760 onwards. It was published in Hone's Year Book. All the names are listed here as '1760*', as the writer gives no dates, but describes them as regular attenders.

2. The Cambridge newspapers. The dates given are those when the merchant first advertised. Some businesses advertised several years running, some intermittently, some only once. Not all the newspapers survive over this period, and there are gaps between 1745 and 1763.

Non-Cambridge businesses:

Adams	Clog & patten maker	Shoreditch, London	1760*
Banks, Wm	Potter	Stoke, Staffs	1768
Barrow	Linen, etc.	London	1794
Birch, Marriott & Mathers	Weavers and Mercers	Fleet Street, London	1765
Bolt	Laceman	Sidney's Alley, London?	1760*
Buttey, Wm	Potter	Ely, Cambs	1768
Carter	Silk Manufacturer	Chandois St, London	1768
Chase, John	Silk Mercer	Long Acre, London	1766
Clark	Linen Draper	Leicester	1773
Clayton, I M & G	Wholesale Leathersellers	Strand, London	1800
Clifton	Millinery	Shoreditch, London	1765
Cockerton, Edward	Oilman	Newgate, London	1787
Cook, John	(previously Jonas Phillips)		1770
Corneck	Hosier	London/Nottingham	1764
Cox & Grossmith	(previously Herne & Cox)		1773
Crowder, Wm	Canes & sticks	Bunhill Row, London	1802
Cuff & Co	Cheesemongers	Whitechapel, London	1794
Doig, James	Gauzes and lawns	Wood St, London	1764
Doolan & Co	Upholsterers	Southwark, London	1769

Fowler	Farming Implements	Shefford, Bedfordshire	1760*
Grainger, J	Tailor & Man's Mercer	Fleet Market, London	1794
Green	Oils and pickles	Limehouse, London	1780s
Haynes	'Norwich Warehouse'	Holborn, London	1760*
Heath, George	Brazier	London	1759
Herne & Cox	Silk Manufacturers	High Holborn, London	1764
Hewitt	Toyman	Smithfield, London	1760*
Jones & Co	Mercery	London	1794
Keene & Co	Fabrics	Clapham	1765
Kelly, J	Harness & Saddlery	Strand, London	1794
Knights, P J	Shawls	Norwich & London	1795
Lacy	Hosier	Clement's Inn, London	1760*
Lany	Laceman	Tavistock St, London	1760*
Lownds, George	Earthenware	Ely, Cambs	1787
Lownds, John	China and glass	St Ives, Hunts	1793
Lucas, Richard	Potter	Ely, Cambs	1785
Malpas, Wm	Swinton Pottery	Doncaster	1770
Mathison, Richard	Cabinet Goods	Southwark	1770
Miller	Tea, coffee, spices	London	1787
Monnery	Leather and Glover	Southwark, London	1760*
Murray	Shoemaker	Bishopsgate, London	1760*
Musgrave, Wm	Draper & Tailor	Ludgate Hill, London	1760s
Oake, Mrs	Milliner	London	
Oswald, John	Bookseller	Poultry, London	1745
Norris, W	Silk Mercer	Covent Gdn, London	1791
Payce, Wm & Son	Tea Warehouse	Smithfield, London	1745
Payce, James	Tea Warehouse	Bloomsbury	1749
Parr	Linen draper	Piccadilly, London	1789
Peat, Thomas	Book & Printseller	Fleet Street, London	1765
Phillips, Jonas	Glass	Norwich, Norfolk	1755
Price, Thomas	Cheese	?	1770
Richardson & Stevenson	Rum Warehouse	Bishopsgate, London	1779
Roake, John	Ironmonger	Wood Street, London	1772
Robinson, Jas	Whips & canes	Thrapston, Northants	1802
Scandrett & Smith	Mercers	London	1758
Smith	Silversmith	Cornhill, London	1760*
Smith, Abraham	Razors & knives	Temple Bar, London	1765
Smith, Anthony	Silk Mercer	Fleet Street, London	1775
Smith, Thomas	Shoemaker	Southwark, London	1764
Spilsbury	Mercer	London	1756

Stretton	Hosier	Nottingham/London	1764
Strickland	Japanned goods	St John's St, London	1793
Thornton, J	Draper	?	1756
Timewell	Milliner	Tavistock St, London	1760*
Troy and Phipps	Mercers	Ludgate Street, London	1751
Tustian, Wm	Cabinet-maker	Whitechapel, London	1760*
Walker, Thomas	Potter	Stoke, Staffs	1773
Ward	Whip-maker	Southwark, London	1760*
Webster	Silks	Tavistock St, London	1769
Wheatley	Silks	Covent Gdn, London	1783
Williams	Cloaks and bonnets	Lombard St, London	1794
Williams & Co	Saddlery	Bloomsbury, London	1759
Williams, G	Saddler	Gt Queen St, London	1764
Wilson	Toyman	Charing Cross, London	1760*
Wilson, Thomas	Potter	Ely, Cambs	1768
Wise & Huson	Mercery	Ludgate St, London	1779
Wood, B	Cheesemonger	Bishopsgate St London	1772
Wright, Jon	Jeweller/hardwareman	Whitechapel, London	1783

The records of Savill of Bocking, clothier, name many wool sellers from the East Midlands.

Sources and Select Bibliography

Cambridgeshire Archives holds the Cambridge Corporation archive, which includes the Common Day Book, booth leases, Pie Powder Court records, etc. and private family archives, such as Baumgartner and Hynde Cotton, which contain Fair information.

The Cambridgeshire Collection in the Cambridge Central Library holds most of the Cambridge newspapers from 1762 onwards and other printed material, as well as maps, guidebooks and directories from the 18th century onwards.

Maitland Robinson Library, Downing College, Bowtell Collection – the notes, papers and manuscript *History of Cambridge* of John Bowtell, bookbinder of Cambridge, who died in 1813. The collection includes Howland Nutting's survey of the Fair in 1711.

Cambridge University Library holds the University Archive, which contains the records of the University's courts held at the Fair, and related documents. The Library also holds some of the early Cambridge newspapers and microfilm of others, such as the *Northampton Mercury*.

The British Library holds the extensive writings of William Cole – information on his contemporaries in 18th century Cambridge, as well as assorted historical notes. (G J Gray: *Index to the contents of the Cole Manuscripts*, 1912, reprinted 2003 is useful.) The British Library Newspaper Collection holds some other editions of the early Cambridge newspapers.

The National Archives' Access to Archives (a2a) database comes up with many Stourbridge references and may disclose more as it grows. *http://www.nationalarchives.gov.uk/a2a/* It's essential to check that references are not to Stourbridge in the West Midlands, and to search using some of the variant spellings of Stourbridge.

References to Stourbridge Fair crop up in so many other diverse places it's impossible to list them here, and I am grateful to the many people who have forwarded them to me.

C H Cooper, *Annals of Cambridge* vols 1–5, Cambridge 1852–, reprinted Cambridge University Press, 2009.

Daniel Defoe, *A Tour through the Whole Island of Great Britain*, first published 1724–6, Penguin edition, edited Pat Rogers, 1971.

Henry Gunning, *Reminiscences ... of Cambridge*, George Bell, London, 1855.

C H Jones, *The Chapel of Saint Mary Magdalene at Sturbridge Cambridge*, Cambridge University Press, 1927.

John S Lee, *Cambridge and its Economic Region 1450–-1560*, University of Hertfordshire Press, 2005.

Tania McIntosh, *The Decline of Stourbridge Fair, 1770–1934*, Friends of the Department of English Local History, University of Leicester, 1998.

G C Moore Smith *"The Refusal of the Hand" A Mock-heroical Poem*, article in Library, June 1922. The original MS of the poem is in the British Library and a printed version (*Stirbitch Fair A Mock-Heroic Poem*) is in the Bodleian Library.

J Nichols, *The history and antiquities of Barnwell Abbey and of Sturbridge Fair*, Biblioteca Topographica Britannica, no XXXVIII, London, 1786. Thomas Hill, *Nundinae Sturbrigiensis*, 1702 (I am very grateful to Marcus Bennet for a translation of this poem.)

W M Palmer ed, *Cambridge Borough Documents Vol I*, Bowes and Bowes, Cambridge, 1931.

Index

People attending the Fair

Alexander, Nicholas 53
Astley's Show 69
Banks, William 45
Bentley, Dr Richard 67
Betson P and J 53
Blaker, Henry 57
Bridgeman, Giles 49
Bridges, Henry 61
Bryene, Alice de 3
Brittan, Jacob 45, 55
Brunton, John 68
Bullman, James 58
Buxton, John 36
Chapman family 79, 80
Chater, Josiah 87
Clappam, Hugh 74
Cook, John 45
Cooper, Richard 32
Corneck, hosier 43
Corsican Fairy, The 57
Cotton, Sir John 76
Crackenthorpe, Rev J 43
Cross, William 59
Cumberland, Richard 68
Davidson, Mr, of London 71
Defoe, Daniel 5, 31, 33-4, 45, 57, 70, 76, 79, 83
Doggett, Thomas 66
Doolan of Southwark 38
Farmer, Dr Richard 68
Female Colossus, The 58
Finch, ironfounders 16, 35
Fox, John 37
Frohock, John 25

Gamble, Richard 32
Gauden, Stephen 58
Gibson, John 40
Goodhall's Music Booth 63
Gray, Thomas 8
Green of Limehouse 23,
Gunning, Henry 56
Gutteridge, Bart. 49
Hardy, Sam 62
Harwood Mr, of Ely 70
Hawtin, Miss 58
Haynes from Holborn 23
Herne and Cox 41
Hill, Thomas 5, 62
Jackson, Stephen
Josselin, Ralph 35, 46
Kelly, J of London 51
Kerrich, Thomas 87, 90
Kettle, Joseph 67
Keynes, Florence 90
King, Thomas 22
Larkin, Elijah 89
Limping Chicken, The 74
MacCragh, Cornelius 58
Mathison, Richard 37
Miles, James 62
Miller, Mr 41
Morgan, Margaret 57
Moses, Judah 44
Musgrave, William 42
Newling, Thomas 40
Newling, William 66
Newton, Isaac 39
Newton, Samuel 80
Nicholson, John 'Maps' 39

Nugent, Richard of Salford 33
Nutting family 13, 76,78, 83
O'Burne, Mr 58
Oswald, John, of London 72
Parratt, Miss T M 16, 76, 82
Philips, Jonas 45, 51
Pidcock, Mr 59
Pinchbeck, C and J 59, 61
Percy, Francis 82
Rayner, Mr 63
Robert, Stephen 32
Roberts, Wm of Marsden 33
Robson, Mr 76
Romilly, Joseph 89
Savill, clothiers 23, 34
Sewster family 54, 82,
Shepherd, John 32
Shepherd, R 64
Smith, Thomas of London 43
Smith, Thomas of Cambridge 16
Sussex Band 63
Sylvesters' waxworks 60
Tustian, William 37-8
Valiant, Joseph 36
Ward, Ned 5, 8, 28, 39, 53, 62, 70, 74
Watson, William 25
Whittred, King 84
Whittlesea, Stephen 24
Whyat, Zachariah, 71

Other aspects of the Fair

Bailiffs 10, 15-18, 26, 55, 84
Barnwell 2, 15, 22, 33, 74
Chesterton 3, 22, 53, 76
Coffee Booth 54-55, 58, 80
Duddery 18, 33, 83, 88
Elizabeth I's charter 5, 76
Garlic Fair 2
Hackney coaches 25, 83
Highwaymen 71
Initiation Rite 28
Learned animals 59
Leper Chapel iv, 5, 15-16, 30, 87, 90
Lord Taps 12, 28
Maypole 18, 26, 83
Microcosm 61
Midsummer Fair 2
Norwich Company 68-69
Oysters 49, 54
Oyster House 51, 56, 88, 90
Panopticon 61
Prostitution 73-74
Pulpit 18, 30
Pye Powder Court 24, 72
Raffling Booth 27, 65-66
Reach Fair 2
Redcoats 12, 25, 55, 72
Regulators 12
Refusal of the Hand 5, 26, 65-66
Robin Hood Booth 27
Saddler's Wells 62-64, 85
'Siegehouse' 18
Step to Stir-Bitch-Fair see Ward, Ned
Thaumasticon 59
Thefts 39, 70-73
University courts 12, 23-24, 32, 36, 38, 40, 46,48-49, 53, 61-62, 74

Money Conversion

Pre-decimal coinage

12d (12 pence) = 1s (1 shilling)

20s = £1 (240d = £1)

1 guinea = £1 1s

Inflation across the centuries and the modern high standard of living make it very difficult to compare sums of money in the past with present-day values.

In the Middle Ages in England, the basic coin was the silver penny. Labourers might earn 2d – 4d a day, but they might also have other resources, such as land for growing crops and raising a few animals.

In Tudor times, skilled craftsmen's wages rose from 6d a day to 1s by the end of the century, so a possible 6s a week.

In the middle of the eighteenth century, a skilled craftsman could earn 12s – 15s a week in London and less in the provinces. His money would go on rent, food, fuel and candles and occasional clothes. If he had a family, there would be only a little left each week for extras.

Thanks and Acknowledgements

Thanks

Many thanks to the staff, past and present, of the Cambridgeshire Archives and the Cambridgeshire Collection for their invaluable help, support and contributions and also to the many local historians and others who have passed on information about the Fair found in the course of their own researches. And thanks to my family for putting up with this project for so long.

Acknowledgements
Thanks to the following for permission to reproduce:
Mrs Brittle p65, Image courtesy of Tunbridge Wells Museum and Art Gallery
Plan of the Fair p81, from *Hone's Year Book* (XIX.55.8). Reproduced by kind permission of the Syndics of Cambridge University Library
Cambridgeshire Collection, Cambridgeshire Libraries, for the cover drawing of the Fair (1820s back to 1760s) and the illustrations on pp 3, 22, 32, 42, 68, 69 and 88
The Pepys Library, Magdalene College, Cambridge for the ballad on p74
The Master, Fellows, and Scholars of Downing College in the University of Cambridge for details p20 from the Bowtell Collection in the Maitland Robinson Library
The Cambridgeshire Records Society for the note from Romilly's Diary p89
Cambridgeshire Archives for the extract from Cambridge Common Day Book p79
Cambridge Past Present and Future for the photo on p91
Other photographs are by the author.